From Mini
To
Millionaire

From Mini To Millionaire

Financial Freedom Is Just A Mindset Away

RIKY ASH

The Choir Press

Copyright © 2026 Riky Ash

All rights reserved. No part of this publication may be reproduced or transmitted in any form or by any means, electronic or mechanical including photocopying, recording or any information storage or retrieval system, without prior permission in writing from the publishers.

The right of Riky Ash to be identified as the author of this work has been asserted by him in accordance with the Copyright, Designs and Patents Act 1988

First published in the United Kingdom in 2026 by

The Choir Press

ISBN 978-1-78963-569-0

From Mini To Millionaire Is Dedicated to an Amazing Man, without Whose Help and Support Since 1992 I Would Not Have the Best Life One Could Possibly Wish For.

That Man Is John Barclay, Equity's Assistant General Secretary.

Thank You, John.

You Made It Happen!

Contents

Introduction ix
How To Make This Book Work for You xi

Chapter 1 - Little Richard 1
Chapter 2 - Hello Mini 9
Chapter 3 - Tell Me About Yourself 18
Chapter 4 - Visualisation 25
Chapter 5 - Cars and Girls 30
Chapter 6 - The Hard Way 36
Chapter 7 - Moving On 40
Chapter 8 - Know Your Worth 45
Chapter 9 - You Have to Make It Happen 50
Chapter 10 - Disciplined – Determined – Dedicated 55
Chapter 11 - Residual Income 63
Chapter 12 - Money Makes Money 68
Chapter 13 - Picks and Shovels 73
Chapter 14 - Cash Is King and Always Will Be 76
Chapter 15 - Prepare Yourself 81
Chapter 16 - The Dangers of Debt 89
Chapter 17 - Multiple Income Streams 93
Chapter 18 - Surround Yourself with Success 98
Chapter 19 - Riky X 101
Chapter 20 - Attitude Is Everything 107
Chapter 21 - The Pension Trap 126
Chapter 22 - You Can Take a Horse to Water 131
Chapter 23 - You Are Your BEST Investment! 140

Introduction

Two shoe salesmen go to Africa. One telephones his manager and says, 'What a wasted journey, no one here wears shoes.'

The second shoe salesman telephones his manager and says, 'Fantastic opportunity, everyone needs shoes.'

Same scenario viewed from differing perspectives. One salesman was negative about the situation he encountered; the other salesman saw an opportunity.

You have to seek those opportunities; they are always out there.

In my life, from a very early age I knew I would be not only successful I would be Super Successful. I thought differently from other children, I played differently and I acted differently. I was mentally and physically tough. My view of the world when growing up in the 1970s was a positive one. Even as a child I saw opportunities all around me.

I was not born into wealth. Mum worked for a time in the world-famous Raleigh bicycle factory, and then in a fish and chip shop by day and as a waitress in a restaurant by night. Dad worked in the famous Nottingham lace industry, and later became self-employed as a market trader, and a very unsuccessful one at that.

Dad was a pathetic businessman and Mum would always advise him what was best. He would then go and do the opposite, which always resulted in failure. Mum had what Dad lacked, Common Sense. Interestingly what most people lack in today's society.

Looking back to those days, I can now establish that my dad had no business acumen. He purchased a derelict corner shop in a residential street in Bulwell, which was a very poor district, to sell fabrics. A fish and chip shop on one corner, and an off-licence on the other, and in between them both was our fabric shop in a rundown part of Nottingham. Mum

Introduction

informed him it was the wrong area for such a shop, and that it would not work. Did he listen? Maybe he did. Did he heed Mum's common-sense advice? No, he went on to make one of the many financial mistakes and bad business decisions of his life.

As Mum correctly predicted, the shop failed and our time in Bulwell was very short-lived.

I learned from a very young age that I was much smarter than most people when it came to money. Even to this very day it still amazes me just how clueless most human beings are when it comes to finance.

From a boy who struggled at school to read, write and do mathematics, I became one of the most successful Stuntmen in the world today, and a Millionaire.

This is my story of how I achieved great wealth, and how you can too. What makes my story so unique is that I have never borrowed money or obtained a loan in my life. In fact, I am against borrowing money and accumulating debt of any kind.

I will take this opportunity to highlight a very interesting characteristic about my personality. I never swear, even though I have used profanities consistently throughout my book for very good reason; to emphasise a point. Vocalising my thoughts carries much greater impact and resonates more strongly with you, the reader. I write all my books in this style.

Read on and you will learn that becoming a Millionaire today is much easier than you think.

How to make this book work for **YOU!**

Throughout my life from a very early age I have been an advocate of being prepared. It is even the Cub Scout motto: "Be Prepared".

I attribute my great success to having this very asset.

For many years now I have made lists. Each night I write a list of objectives, both business and personal. I am organised and reliable, have a photographic memory and like an elephant, I never forget.

To make using this book easy for you I have highlighted Vital Points which I emphasise with the words **Write It Down.**

The most successful Millionaires, Multimillionaires and Billionaires are organised. We all have the same traits, we make lists, we keep notes, we write information down. If we did not possess this attribute, we would not have created our considerable wealth.

By writing valuable information down in a book, yes you read that correctly, a book, it frees up your mind to focus on other financial ventures and allows you a collated resource to refer back to when required.

Now get yourself a notebook and label it as follows:

From '   ' to Millionaire'.

It could be 'From Cleaner to Millionaire'.

Your name to Millionaire.

'From £300 to Millionaire'.

'From Broke to Millionaire'. The choice is yours.

Remember "Be Prepared" – **Write It Down.**

How to make this book work for YOU!

I do not want you to use any form of technology like a computer or a smart phone, write only in a book with a pencil or pen.

Everything you require to become a Millionaire is contained within these pages. However I MUST stress you will have to WORK HARD. Nothing worth having in life comes to us that easily, you MUST be prepared to WORK HARD, if not you WILL FAIL.

You will encounter knockbacks along the way, that is life and in life, it is not the number of punches you can throw, it is the number you are able to take that will form you.

No one has ever succeeded at anything without first encountering failure. Through failure we either give up or succeed, we give up or we find a way. Confident individuals are Positive individuals. We always find a way.

Provided you work hard, you WILL find a way to succeed and become a Millionaire.

Through hard work and self-belief I took myself from working at a backstreet cabinetmaker's workshop in Netherfield, Nottingham, to becoming a world-famous Millionaire Stuntman.

This is how I achieved it.

Read on and enjoy.

Chapter 1

Little Richard

From a very young age I knew I was going to be successful. Why? Because I was always positive. I was a slow learner and struggled at school. My father was a very violent man and better described as a failure, a very irresponsible businessman. Mum, however, was completely the opposite; she lacked a formal education, having been born and schooled in the strict Roman Catholic education system in Southern Ireland. Regardless, Mum was sharp as a pin and as I write this in 2024 at the age of eighty, she still is.

I strongly believe that our childhood is our foundation for our future, that by the age of seven our personalities are formed. My personality was one of success. Even as a child I believed so much in myself and my actions that I convinced myself I could not and would not fail. I am so pleased that today, only weeks away from my 57th birthday, I still adopt that attitude no matter what, because it works.

I can never lose, I can never fail, I either win or learn.

I was never a child who had friends, I was never one of the crowd or a team player, and realised at a very early age in life that I would be ostracised no matter what. This had no effect on me as I just used it as Fuel for My Fire. You will see those words occur and recur throughout my book for good reason.

I was born in the famous Meadows area of Nottingham, at home on 30 August 1967. We moved from The Meadows to Cropwell Terrace in Hyson Green, Nottingham. It was a back-to-back house with a front yard, no bathroom, just two bedrooms, a very small kitchen and a lounge. Mum would bathe my brother and me in the kitchen sink, while my parents would attend what was referred to as "the Baths", a communal place where one paid to use the washing facilities.

Cropwell Terrace was one of the most rundown and deprived back-to-back houses in England. Mum could never understand why Dad sold a very practical house to relocate to a street that would have been condemned back in the 1800s. How interesting that today we have gone full circle, with developers being allowed by very irresponsible councils all over England to yet again build tomorrow's slums in the name of greed.

As far back as 1973 I remember my father saying that I would only end up sweeping the streets. Now I have to stress a point here and a very valuable one; even if I had become a street cleaner that is no bad job, our street cleaners do an excellent job and a vital job at that, so I have no idea what my father was implying when he made that pathetic statement.

My father was very strict; when I say strict, I mean strict. Today his behaviour would warrant a long prison sentence. He ruled with a steel rod, that rod was the metal tubing from our vacuum cleaner.

He believed in hitting and hitting hard, not only to instil strict discipline, but also to make me learn, which massively backfired as I then developed a hatred for learning and became somewhat remedial. It was not the fact that I did not want to learn, it was the fear of trying to learn and making a mistake which brought pain.

In the long summer holidays, he would mark several pages of a book and insist I read it, asking me a series of questions on his return from work. He did not believe in a child playing and enjoying their summer holidays. I would always read the pages that were set for me and spend the rest of the day dreading his return from work, tired and moody, ready to take his anger out on me.

I would be asked, "What colour was the farmer's dog?" If I got the answer wrong, I was hit and hit very hard with the metal vacuum cleaner tube. This would continue throughout the asking of each question, normally ten or twelve of them. Some I got right, most I got wrong, so a beating I received each time. I always remember being beaten so hard that I would wet myself then get beaten again for that.

As appalling as those early days of my life were, they formed me, they made me the strong, confident person I am today, because my father did not believe in his own son and did not believe I would be successful. Because I was small for my age, he wrote me off as a complete failure, which created the Fuel for My Fire attitude.

I believe attitude is everything to becoming successful and wealthy.

Attitude Is Everything – **Write It Down.**

If you do not adopt the correct attitude you will fail. In all aspects of life, Attitude Is Everything, the attitude you adopt to becoming super successful and a Millionaire has to be a positive one.

My parents did not believe in giving a child pocket money. On those very rare occasions when my brother and I were given 10 pence by Mum, my brother would go straight to the ice-cream van. The 10 pence I was given would go straight into my savings box. From a very early age I saved, whereas my brother spent. I was only five and even at such a young age I appreciated the value of money and that putting the occasional 10 pence into my savings box resulted in the ten pences becoming one pound.

My savings box was filling up while my brother's box remained empty.

We were brought up to work and by that, I mean work. I began working at the age of seven, which would involve loading our van for the weekend markets, where my parents worked with their fabric stall throughout the 1970s.

We were not rich; my dad's attitude towards money was that it was everything in life and nothing else mattered. When our washing machine broke, Dad would not purchase a new one for Mum, demanding that she wash our clothes in the sink. Everything purchased was secondhand, this was the norm throughout the 1970s as products were very expensive and wages low.

Throughout the week Dad worked as a manager for a bleachers and dyers and lace manufacturer by the name of Hicking and Pentecost. Lace from Nottingham was famous the world over. Mum worked as a dinner lady at my first ever school, Southwalk Street, in Basford, Nottingham. Mum gave my brother and me as much as she could, as my Dad did not even believe in giving a child birthday or Christmas presents.

Mum was positive, Dad was negative. I was able to establish from a very young age that by being positive, better things happened, and one lived a much happier life.

I knew I was different from other children. I was always happy, despite having a violent father who beat me on a near-daily basis. I had a very positive outlook upon life even as a child and possessed a quality that even adults today do not have; I have no fear of anything, there is absolutely nothing on this planet that scares me. I am without question the bravest person ever to have lived and I really do mean that. I had no idea that as a child this was going to be an amazing asset to my chosen career as a Stuntman.

From a very young age I loved cars. When finances allowed, Mum would buy my brother and me a bar of chocolate and a Matchbox car from the local newsagent next to our school.

I loved those very rare days. We would always know that Mum was going to do this as we would walk a different way towards the shops. My chocolate bar of choice was Aero, and I got to choose what Matchbox car I liked.

I still have those cars today, not carrying any great value as I played with them and I believe all children should. It is often said that if one had kept the collection pristine and with the original box they would be worth hundreds, if not thousands, of pounds today.

It was the 1970s and parents and children did not think that way. If any astute parent had, they would have purchased duplicates, one for the child to play with and the other as an investment.

What we must never do is say, What If – **Write It Down.**

It is vitally important that you do not have regrets when it comes to finance.

You will Win or Learn. – **Write It Down.**

You will never lose if you learn.

That smart boy from Nottingham was creating a foundation for a very successful future, when other children were only focusing on the chimes of the ice-cream van. Even though Mum and many of my neighbours worked for a time at the Raleigh bicycle factory, we could not afford a new bike, so I was presented with a rusty second-hand cycle, with a puncture, known as an RSW 11 Raleigh Small Wheel. Even though it was not new I was still grateful; I was a child who appreciated whatever was given to me.

I set to work as a six-year-old to renovate the bike, with help from Mum, as Dad was totally useless when it came to anything practical. If something needed repairing or decorating in our home, it was Mum that did it.

From an old rusty bicycle came my first experience of freedom, once I had learned to ride it. I had never ridden a bicycle in my life so now was the time to learn. I bolted stabilisers on and was teased by other children who were younger than me who had learned to ride from a much younger age. If my parents had been wealthier and if Dad had not decided that his children should not receive presents, I am sure I would have been bought a bike at a much younger age and would be riding freely without stabilising aids.

When other children laughed at me it made me more determined to progress, to prove them wrong and also to prove me right; no matter what negativity I receive I will always be successful.

Use any negativity that is directed towards you as Fuel for Your Fire – **Write It Down.**

If you take any criticism, or words you may deem as being offensive you will fail. You have to be both mentally and physically tough to survive today.

When we were growing up, along with learning the days of the week, being able to tell the time, read, write and learn our times tables, we were told this:

STICKS AND STONES MAY BREAK MY BONES BUT NAMES WILL NEVER HURT ME.

Write It Down.

This is vital to you becoming successful and if you desire to be a Millionaire, you MUST stop bothering about what other people think of you.

When you read my amazing book, *With Confidence*, which is very direct, I cover comprehensively my thoughts on WOKEism and this pathetic 'Blame Game', 'I've been offended' pathetic society we reside in today.

You have to be better than that, your long road to success is going to be a very ruthless one. If you get offended at being called names, give up now as you have already lost.

Even as a child of six I was able to establish that no matter what was said to me no one was ever going to destabilise my happiness and my positive future.

Living in Basford, Nottingham, was one of the most enjoyable times of my childhood. We experienced what was referred to as The Three-Day Week, which was instigated by the then Conservative government to combat the industrial action that deprived the country power stations of coal, resulting in a shortage of electricity, so candles were lit to provide light. Cooking had to be carried out before the electricity was turned off, which was around 10.30pm; by this time Little Richard was fast asleep in bed.

Times were very difficult in the 1970s; children were not demanding, we were grateful to have a meal, some clothes, which were always secondhand, and a bed to sleep in. Today children rule their parents and sadly parents are so weak they allow this.

So if you desire to be a Millionaire you must be Grateful – **Write It Down.**

For whatever I was given I was always grateful; even today as a Millionaire I appreciate the smallest of gifts.

Little Richard was always positive; no matter how bad life could sometimes be, I never believed my situation would always remain that way.

I had a fantastic Mum and a pathetic Dad, positive and negatives combined. Even from a very young age I used a process for success that is better known as visualisation, which I still use to this very day.

Whatever I desired, whatever outcome I envisaged, I would visualise it. Think of it this way. Young children liked to have posters on their bedroom walls of the things that inspired and impressed them, fast cars and bikes, trains, fighter jets, you could even have wallpaper carrying those very images. That is a form of visualisation. Teenage girls would cut out their favourite music and movie stars and plaster their bedroom walls, fantasising that they were their girlfriend, again a form of visualisation.

Super successful people use Vision Boards. A vision board is similar to a notice board placed upon one's wall, to which goals can be pinned.

So now you have a task to create your very own vision board. It can be any size, you can even have several. Cut out photographs of what you desire to achieve and pin them to your board. Every day look at your vision board, look at it several times throughout the day and before you go to bed, look at it again.

Even as a Millionaire I still have a vision board, because if you are an entrepreneur, you still have goals you wish to achieve. Just because you are wealthy do not stop there.

Do Richard Branson and James Dyson still go to work? What about Andrew Tate, earning £21,000,000 in one year? He still rises early every day and works. That is what super successful people do, we work and work hard and even harder, we make millions and enjoy the fact because of our determination to be super successful and work even harder; despite our vast wealth we still work, every waking hour, that is what we do.

We also work smart.

Before you begin Chapter Two you have a task to perform.

You are going to create your Vision Board.

Chapter 2

Hello Mini

In 1976 we moved from Bulwell in Nottingham after one of my dad's many business ventures failed yet again, to a new private housing estate by the name of Rise Park. Ironically this house was repossessed in 1999, again because of my dad's appalling track record of having no business acumen whatsoever.

I was to reside there throughout the remainder of my school days, into my working life after leaving Top Valley Comprehensive School in 1983 and on to becoming a Stuntman in 1993.

I attended the newly built Rise Park Junior School, which was walking distance from home. Rise Park estate was different, everyone had a garage and a driveway, and most people had decent cars, and new cars at that. We seemed to be doing well, new house and new car, everyone seemed to be enjoying the trappings of success. However, from the outside looking in, one would think everyone was wealthy but the only people who were wealthy were the money lenders. We were racked by debt, everyone was, mortgage and car finance.

I must stress a valid point; debt back then was not given out as easily as it is today, when a teenager can obtain finance for a new car with an interest rate of 1%.

Life was just not like that in the 1970s, the interest rate was around 14%.

Now as you are aware, I created my vast wealth without ever taking out a loan. I DO NOT believe in borrowing money, I DO NOT believe in mortgages, as that is borrowing money.

Ask most people who owns the house and they will say they do, when the real answer should be the bank. Unless they do not have a mortgage, the bank owns it.

I never believed in borrowing money, I never received pocket money, and every penny mattered to me. To date I have never had a loan or mortgage, and I never will.

Never borrow money, NEVER – **Write It Down.**

If you have borrowed money and are in any form of debt, WHY? What did you need that was so vital that you had to get yourself into debt? You need to do everything possible to repay that debt and never borrow money again.

You will read in later chapters the importance of NOT borrowing money, EVER!

1978 was the year of one of the many turning points in my life, as my dad left my mum; not only did he leave her emotionally, he left her in such a financial mess that it was disgraceful to witness. What a ruthless, selfish and evil man he was.

From a ten-year-old's eyes, I saw other children having so much fun and enjoying their childhood but mine was witnessing Mum struggling to pay the bills and put food on the table. When Dad left he took absolutely everything, cutlery out of the kitchen drawers, furniture, bedding, the only item he did not take was our television, because it belonged to Radio Rentals. In the 1970s very few households could afford a new television, so it became common to rent. Mum had to prioritise and our rental television had to be returned as it was an expense Mum could do without.

Even though Mum did her very best to provide, food was very expensive. I took to foraging out of bins for extra nourishment. I would stand outside the shopping precinct in Rise Park and wait until someone would put their chip wrapper into the bin. I would then go over and take it behind the shops and eat whatever remains the wrapper contained. Life was hard. What this taught me was determination, determination, no matter what, to succeed.

I was never academic although I was not classed as remedial; I could read and write and could do very basic maths. However, my father's strict way to try to make me learn by beating me with the metal part of our vacuum cleaner made me rebel against any form of education, so I struggled.

I never had many friends at school; I was not one of the crowd. I established from a very early age that I was an individual and would never be a team player. This I used to my great advantage as I got older and much wiser.

It was at school in 1977 that I was given the nickname of Mini because of my very small stature, which was due to being malnourished.

For all the negatives of my early childhood, I did not realise that being short – if you did not already know I am only 5 feet 3 inches inches tall – would become a great asset to my career as a Stuntman.

When I informed my fiancée, Katrina, that I was referred to as Mini because I was so small, she said that would be a great title for my finance book. So now you know the origins of *From Mini to Millionaire*.

No one called me Richard anymore, I was known as Mini and this nickname stuck for many years. A long-lost friend who now resides in New Zealand sent me an email last year saying, "Hello Mini." I had not heard that for many years, and it brought back memories of my childhood and teenage days.

So as a child who never received pocket money, witnessed his mother struggling financially, was beaten on a near-daily basis by an aggressive father and was very rarely bought toys or treats, I knew what hardships felt like, from living it on a daily basis.

I knew that no matter what, I was going to be successful.

Never allow past negative experiences to define your future – **Write It Down.**

I hated every second of my comprehensive school days. In 1978 I started my secondary education at Top Valley Comprehensive School. Apart from home life when my dad was living with us, this was the first time I really experienced negativity. I hated every day of life at Top Valley but despite this, my attendance was exemplary. Not being a team player means you become ostracised; however, this gave me a solid foundation for my life as a Stuntman, where I have also been ostracised, alongside being hated. Does it bother me? No, why should it? Nothing Ruffles My Feathers.

Remember in life if you desire to be Super Successful and a Multi-Millionaire sadly you will make enemies.

You are going to read these very words regularly throughout all my writing and they must resonate with you.

I judge my success not by how many people like me but by how many people actually dislike me. I know that most people dislike a very successful person; therefore, I know the more people dislike me, the more I am doing things right.

I have never wanted to fit in; I was born to stand out.

I ONLY HAVE TO JUSTIFY MY ACTIONS TO MYSELF

The only lessons I really enjoyed at school were drama and woodwork. I wanted to be an actor or a carpenter. Ironically, I achieved both. Whatever I have set out to achieve throughout my life I have, despite all the negativity that has been thrown in my direction.

NEVER allow anyone to dictate your future – **Write It Down.**

Incidentally, how's that vision board coming along? Is it on the wall yet?

Top Valley was a cesspit of negativity. Most children had no intention of learning and bettering themselves, and certainly no intention of ever seeking employment on leaving school. Very few children went to university, which I believe is the correct approach. One should only go to university if the job in question warrants such a direction.

Do not waste your time going to university to acquire a degree which is not fit to Wipe a Tramp's Ass With, be racked in debt, have no common sense and land a job flipping burgers just because our corrupt pathetic no-good government brainwashed you into believing that is what you need to do to become successful.

Let's just look at success for a moment. I am successful, I am Super Successful, I am a Millionaire, do I have a degree? NO. Did I go to university? NO. Am I flipping burgers? NO. Did I allow our corrupt government to brainwash me?

I sure DID NOT.

Do you see university lecturers driving around in Lamborghinis?

This country's education system is shite. When I look back at my school days, compared to the education system of today my generation's education had its flaws; however, it prepared the school leaver for The Real World, not like today, where children are being lied to in that a degree will secure their future.

So, unless your degree is of value, doctor or lawyer, you may as well just wipe your ass with it, because it will not make you rich. To progress to Millionaire status, you MUST reject everything our corrupt government says and tells you – **Write It Down.**

You will read more on that very subject in a later chapter.

Even back in my school days, whenever I said, "I wished to do…" I was always hit with the reply, "No you won't." In 1983, close to my leaving school, we were talking about work; the fact that England was in recession did not mean anything to me because I did not even know what a recession was. What I did know was I would secure employment, no matter what. However, my classmates thought differently with the attitude, "You will sign on like the rest of us." Did I sign on like the rest of them? NO, I disciplined myself to find a job, and that is exactly what I did.

(Just to make you aware, signing on was the process for an unemployed person to receive benefits.)

This was carried out at a local job centre on a fortnightly basis, where one would be required to prove that they were actively seeking employment.

I had no intention whatsoever of doing that, I was destined to work.

Now as you are aware, I came from nothing. At the time of leaving school in 1983 I was still wearing hand-me-down clothes that no longer fitted my brother and even to this day would still be too large for me.

I left school on Friday 27 May 1983; that was it, I had served my sentence at Top Valley Comprehensive School and hated every second of it. The reality is that you cannot change life. However, you can change your mind, and how you react.

Ask yourself this: What Is Your Current Mindset Bringing You?

I hated the people I had to sit in class with. I hated the education system. If I had known then what I know now I would have left home and joined the circus, or got a job with Mr Kipling, filling tarts with cream.

I always enjoyed working with wood and my ambition was to become a carpenter. For my tenth birthday my parents bought me a toolbox. I still have that very toolbox today. I was committed to securing employment before I left school. We were encouraged to write to around 25 businesses in Nottingham to increase our chances of securing work, bearing in mind that other school leavers would be doing the same.

It was a difficult time in which to secure a job back then as we were in the depths of high unemployment in 1983. I do not think I would be inaccurate in stating that there would only be around five woodworking businesses in the city today, if that.

I was determined to progress whereas other children were not. At school, when we had established what job we wished to realistically do and had written the 25 letters to the various companies in the Nottingham area, we had to include with those letters a stamped addressed envelope. There was a fatal flaw with this one. Mum was struggling to put food on the table and had no additional funds for stationery and stamps. I had set my sights on becoming a carpenter and nothing was going to stop me.

No way was this going to deter me, so, what I did was use a quality that I still use to this every day, DETERMINATION. No matter what, I never give up, I never lose, I only learn.

I wrote my job applications onto file paper I obtained from school and was fortunate to be given some envelopes by Mum. Letters written, with no stamps, I walked from my home in Rise Park several miles across the city to post my letters in the business letterboxes over several evenings through all weathers. How many children would do that today? How many children today have it in them to work hard and become a Millionaire?

Throughout my book I will keep stressing the value of working hard and hard work. Nothing, absolutely nothing in life worth having comes to you easily – **Write It Down.**

Out of the 25 letters I hand-delivered, only two replied and both stated that they were not taking on any apprentices that year. This did not deter me, as I knew no matter what I would secure employment and be super successful, because I was DETERMINED. So I enrolled on a Youth Training Scheme, set up by the government to allow school leavers an opportunity to gain employment for one year, earning £25 per week, which today (2024) would be £105 which, ironically, was the exact figure I was earning in 1990 when I left my cabinet making job at Thomas Pearson.

Now, for a child of 15 who never received pocket money, having £25 paid to me in cash every Friday was amazing. I gave Mum £10 for board which left me with £15. I was still able to travel on Nottingham buses for 10 pence so getting to work cost me £1 per week, so in my mind I was loaded.

The first treat I ever bought myself was a Webley Tempest .22 Air Pistol. It cost me £45. Back in 1983 £45 was a lot of money for one to have. Even as a teenager I used visualisation, something I still do to this very day. I had pictures of a Webley Tempest air pistol, which I had cut out of an air gun magazine, blue tacked to my bedroom wall, knowing that one day I would own one. I so wanted the Webley Tempest air pistol and saved hard for it. I still have that very air pistol today, still working and in excellent condition. I will never part with it, as to me it represents that working hard and smart equates to reward.

How is your Vision Board progressing?

What I really needed to purchase was tools, as every tradesman must have his own set.

No matter how wealthy I am, I still value the possessions I purchased in my teenage years and still today could take you into my workshop and show you tools which are now over 40 years old. I look after everything I own and am always grateful. Even as a small child I was grateful for anything I was given and I still am today.

Even working on a YTS and only being paid £25 per week I saved, I saved what little I had; at this point I did not have a bank or building society account, so I kept my savings at home.

Every Sunday I would count my money. It was a great feeling knowing that through hard work I was seeing results, even though very small as far as income was concerned; however, I was working.

I worked in Hucknall, a part of Nottingham which is the famous resting place of George Byron, commonly known as Lord Byron, as a joiner for a self-employed builder who taught me more about drinking and womanising than I learned about joinery and construction. This was amazing for a sixteen-year-old boy. I did, however, learn a little about the construction industry. I will never forget just how much time this married man spent in the pub or in several women's knickers, as I was often sent to the DIY shop for long stands and short weights.

Chapter 3

Tell Me About Yourself

I had just turned 16. I was astute enough to understand that the Youth Training Scheme only afforded you one year of security; once the year had expired one was back looking for more secure employment. As much as I enjoyed working in Hucknall there was no guarantee that I would be taken on full-time, once my one-year contract expired. I began looking in the local newspaper employment section. In February of 1984 I was reading through the employment opportunities in the *Nottingham Evening Post* and noticed a job advertised for the position of Trainee Cabinet Maker in Netherfield, Nottingham. I was required to write a letter to a Post Office Box number, which I did.

Some days later I received a telephone call from the company owner, John Pearson, asking me if I was available to attend an interview.

On that day John's first question was, "Tell me about yourself." Now we had rehearsed interview techniques at school; however, we were never briefed on that one, again demonstrating just how pathetic school actually is. I relaxed and began with a conversation about my passion for woodwork which led onto my time serving in the Air Training Corps (ATC).

I had joined the ATC in 1982 and loved every second of it. I spoke fondly of my dedication to the ATC and the vital skills I had learned alongside discipline.

To become a Millionaire you will need to be Disciplined – **Write It Down.**

I was unaware that John Pearson had been a captain in the army; he had seen active service and respected the discipline that the military instilled in a person. The interview became a very relaxed affair, and I was telephoned by John that evening and offered the position. As pleased as I was to be offered this job, informing my previous employer was a daunting experience, as I knew he would be sad to see me leave – more for the cover-up stories I had provided him with for his unacceptable behaviour.

If I had not been proactive about regularly checking the job advertisements in the *Nottingham Evening Post*, I would not have seen the job advertised.

I Made It Happen!

Whatever you desire in life you MUST Make It Happen – **Write It Down.**

I started at Thomas Pearson on Monday 5 March 1984, which was the beginning of the coal miners' strike. My salary was £45 per week. I was now £20 a week better off.

So let's just go back to that day at Top Valley Comprehensive School when my classmates said, "You will sign on like the rest of us." Did I sign on? No, I was dedicated and had the self-belief NOT to be influenced in any way by toxicity.

To become a Millionaire, you MUST have Self-belief – **Write It Down.** Despite my wages rising, my board was increased from £10 per week to £15. I also gave Miserable Nev £2 per week to provide me with a lift each morning and afternoon.

Now to obtain that lift to work I had to get up at 6.00am and walk two miles every morning to get a lift from miserable Nev. He was a wood veneerer, a dull individual who lived a negative life. At the end of a hard day, miserable Nev would drop me off in the place he had collected me from and again I would walk two miles home. I did this from 1984 until 1986, five days a week, until I passed my driving test and could afford a car. How many people today would walk four miles in a day to work? My personality has a get on with it attitude, I never moan, **I DO**, I never make excuses, **I DO**.

I Make It Happen. You already have that written down in your book.

Even after giving Mum £15 board and miserable Nev his £2 I was left with £28 at the end of each week. This £28 I saved. I opened a Halifax Building Society and a Nottingham Building Society account and played one against the other as their interest rates fluctuated, which back in 1984 was around 9%.

I have my own view on interest rates. I firmly believe they should never be less than 10%. The only reason they are so low is because our government wants you to be in debt. Now you may say that our corrupt government does not have any control over interest rates; WRONG. They do, do not ever believe that our corrupt government does not have control of our banking system. The lower the interest rate, the more incentive there is for stupid people to borrow money, accumulate debt and then be a slave to the government, attempting to repay. More on that very subject of debt in a later chapter.

My work colleagues laughed at me for saving, as they much preferred to take their weekly wage and hand it straight over to the bartender at the local pub. They were all broke and never contemplated why. I have always been astute and could deduce firstly it was through their negative approach to life and secondly having no ambition whatsoever.

My work colleagues laughed at me when I said I was going to be rich, famous and super successful. They constantly put me down, which created my, 'Nothing Ruffles My Feathers' attitude and an even greater drive to be successful and prove them wrong.

All they lived for was Friday payday so they could go and get pissed over the weekend and then be broke with absolutely nothing to show for it, on returning to work Monday morning. They spent, I saved, they found it highly amusing that a boy of 16 did not want to go out getting pissed, as they put it, preferring to stay home in the evenings and weekends saving.

What they were unaware of was that 16-year-old boy was home at the weekend reading finance books and magazines and preparing himself for a successful life. I never divulged this to them; why would I? They would never have understood, they were not that smart, and were no way as financially astute as I was.

What I really hated was pubs and clubs. Unless you actually own one you are just losing money by frequenting them. Ironically today there is very little income, if any, from investing in the hospitality industry. On a very rare occasion I would go into Nottingham on a Saturday night, and I hated every second of it, a complete waste of money.

I only drank alcohol for nine months of my life, when I was 18, and never drank again. I just saw no positives in drinking piss from the Last Leper in Hell, just like smoking. I want things in my life that make me money, NOT lose me money.

Only invest in those activities that will Make You Money – **Write It Down.**

I am not saying, don't take up a hobby or an interest; what I am saying is ditch the smoking and drinking. The money wasted on such vice can be channelled elsewhere to actually make you money. Remember, you are going to progress to Millionaire status without ever having to take out a loan or borrow money, now how impressive is that?

My first job of the day at Thomas Pearson's was to sweep the workshop floor, followed by the machine shop then onto the veneer shop, ending with the spray shop. This routine took me up to 9.30am when my next task was to collect the snack orders for those that were far too lazy to make their own lunch. A walk to the shops each day was very enjoyable, often getting telephone numbers and dates from the many attractive and some not so attractive girls to smoke in on later.

On one occasion I saw at the time my dream car, a Bertone X1/9, which was very rare. If you have never seen one now is the time to research one of the most amazing cars ever made, carrying the name of the famous automotive designer Nuccio Bertone, who created works of art for both Ferrari and Lamborghini. Ironically it was back in 1983 when working in Hucknall, Nottingham that I saw my first ever X1/9 and I've loved them ever since.

They were marketed through FIAT dealerships. I would visit as many as possible to view them and collect various sales brochures which were then pinned to my vision board. I used the power of visualisation to ensure that one day I would be the very proud owner of a junior supercar.

Now I am going to stress a point. Your personality will dictate whether you will or will not make it to Millionaire status. Each evening, I would make my lunch for the following day. This saved me money, whereas my work colleagues were far too lazy to do this. If one was to calculate how much they spent each week on lunches it would add up to well over a thousand pounds per year, money well wasted. All they were doing was making another person rich. The small purchases add up, and if you adopt a more modest approach to your finances you will make savings in areas that matter.

I see this so much with coffee. Do people really need that morning coffee at £4 per time? No, they do not, so let's do some calculations. Morning coffee at £4 five days a week = £20.00 x that by let's say 40 weeks as one may not have a coffee every day; that equates to a whopping £800, to me a complete waste of money. Now you may not think so yourself and that is purely your choice, however, taking into consideration that a person who purchases the coffee probably purchases a sandwich also, it all adds up and it all matters.

Purchase only what you need NOT what you want – **Write It Down.**

It is vital for every craftsman to have tools; however, cabinet-making tools were very expensive, and one was encouraged to only purchase the best. So, the money accumulating in my savings accounts went towards purchasing my kit. Those very tools I still have today, they have earned their keep and paid for themselves many times over.

There are opportunities all around you – **Write It Down.**

While working at Thomas Pearson I saw an opportunity. There was a substantial amount of timber offcuts which would accumulate. One of my many jobs each day was to cart them into the timber cellar for anyone who required free firewood. Some of the offcuts were usable, so I used them.

I would make boxes out of them to sell, and these became so successful that I was doubling my income each week. Again, every Monday morning I would walk into Netherfield, establishing which building society was paying the best interest, and there my earnings would go. Again, each Monday morning my work colleagues would laugh at me.

Who's Laughing Now!

I have those very words written on my study board; when you become super successful you can have those words written too. They are so true of life; with whatever you aspire to do you will encounter negativity along the way and you now know that you are going to utilise the negative attitudes of others as Fuel for Your Fire to drive you to super success and Millionaire status.

As you are very well aware, Attitude Is Everything. You even have it written in your book.

The attitude I adopted back in the 1980s is the very same attitude I have today, no one is ever going to control my success and future. To be super successful you MUST adopt this attitude, you will eventually become Bullet Proof and will also be able to say, Who's Laughing Now!

In 1988 I made a life-changing decision, taking up Shaolin Kung-Fu, at the time not realising what future opportunities becoming an expert in this fighting art were going to bring. Kung-Fu was my foundation on my long journey to becoming a Millionaire.

A journey well worth the time, effort and very hard painful work.

Chapter 4

Visualisation

The major turning point for me was in 1987, when I was just 19 years old. Why was it that so many people were having so much fun and having the time of their lives at a time when Cash Was King? Why was my life stagnant? I was still working at Thomas Pearson, a fine furniture maker and restorer in Netherfield, Nottingham, as a cabinet maker, earning at the time £75 per week, which is the equivalent of £261 today (2024).

I enjoyed every second of being a cabinet maker, going from Boy to Man experiencing the tough life of the world of work, not the false picture that the Thatcher government were painting. The working and social environment was sexist, racist, homophobic and not politically correct. Not like the pathetic WOKE Snowflake society we sadly reside in today.

Back then Shit4Brainz were not glueing their ugly faces to the M25 in the name of non-existent climate change.

The 1980s were amazing. I could not afford what one would refer to today as a proper driving instructor; I could only afford a Pakistani man by the name of Shaheed. Alongside his dodgy school of motoring, he also ran an off-licence and newsagents. Fair play to the man for trying. However, his car of choice was a 1977 Datsun 120Y and a very poor example, at that.

Now driving lessons were very expensive, which was why I had no choice but to go with Shaheed in his knackered 1977 Datsun for £5 per hourly lesson. Other instructors were charging around £11 per lesson; tests back then were £14.40.

To give you some understanding of just how unroadworthy his car was, on my test the examiner kept asking me what the banging was. The result was a request to pull over where safe and activate my hazard lights so that he could investigate, to discover that the nearside wing was hanging off! Driving test cancelled and a FAIL issued.

Now Shaheed refused to refund me my test fee, and my pathetic father would not go and see him, to redress the balance. At this point in my life, I was not training in Kung-Fu; if I had been, I would have kicked Seven Shades Of Shit out of him and received a refund that way.

I continued learning to drive in Mum's car, taking it out at every opportunity, even driving solo to gain vital experience. I went on to pass my test in Mum's Datsun Cherry, which was more roadworthy than anything Shaheed was using.

I bought a £300 Ford Escort van. It was the best I could afford, no insurance and only the tax and MOT that came with it. The 1980s, for some, represented survival; you did what you needed to do and if that meant not giving our thieving government any more money than they deserved that is exactly what you did. In my mind they deserve nothing for the appalling and irresponsible way they run this country.

To earn extra money, I did what was referred to as 'jobs on the side'. I managed to secure some painting and decorating work in the hot summer of 1987; I secured a contract to redecorate a flat that a landlord was going to rent out in the Mapperley area of Nottingham.

I was up on a stepladder, wallpapering and through the window saw opposite me a Red Ferrari, parked outside a company by the name of Cavendish Finance. On the opposite side of the road a new UPVC window company had opened and parked outside there was a White Porsche 911 Cabriolet. Now most people in Nottingham had never seen these types of cars and the reaction when seeing them was again met with negativity and jealousy. My reaction was always the opposite; I admired people who had worked hard and rightly rewarded themselves. I have always loved Lamborghinis and that day motivated me so much.

I wanted that life. There was I in my £300 van and there were people driving cars worth tens of thousands of pounds; I wanted some. I was astute enough to know that as a cabinet maker I was never going to afford a Lamborghini and afford the amazing life I had set myself. I also understood that the government did not want me to be successful and was my ultimate enemy. Governments are powerless unless you are subservient, and I sure was not going to be anyone's bitch.

My early life was shit, my current life could have been shit, I could have just stagnated and watched everyone else having so much enjoyment; that would have been easy, it would have been easy to stay miserable and have a shit life. I did not want that kind of life, Shit Life, Shit Wife, living in Shitsville. I took action, **I Made It Happen.** I worked on my mind, my mindset, my visualisation of how I wanted my life to look.

The day I saw the Ferrari and the Porsche I visualised what my life would be like, driving my dream car. Now, I have always been realistic and knew that a cabinet-maker's wage was not going to afford me a Lamborghini or even a Bertone X1/9, as in the 1980s Lamborghini customers were either rock stars, movie stars or very successful businessmen. A Lamborghini Countach in 1989 would set you back £75,000 which equates to £261,000 today (2024).

I read Millionaire mindset books, financial magazines and, when everyone else was listening to music, I was listening to motivational and success cassette tapes. I would purposely visit Graypaul Ferrari's dealership in Loughborough at the age of 19 and look at the cars. I would drive past Millionaire mansions and watch documentaries about successful people. I was fascinated with success. When I could obtain a car magazine, I would look at the images and visualise what my life would be like owning a Lamborghini; they were by far the absolute symbol of success, and I was going to have one.

Hard work was instilled into me by my mum, Catherine, who grew up in Southern Ireland with the very strict upbringing that if you wanted anything in life you had to work hard for it.

If you want anything in life you have to work hard for it – **Write It Down.**

I never believed in borrowing money. As you are aware, I never received pocket money, and every penny mattered to me. I was no stranger to hard work, having laboured from the age of seven.

I associated supercars with wealth. My passion was cars, I absolutely loved them; most guys did in the 1980s, so visualisation became a very important part of my life and still is. Even as a working Stuntman, when I receive a telephone call for a job and I read that the script requires me to dive through a window and land down into an airbag, even though I have performed this stunt several times I still visualise doing it. I also visualise what I am going to spend my money on. Even before I was wealthy, I thought like a wealthy person, I would at every opportunity be around wealthy people.

I remember back in 1987 when I first saw a Lamborghini Jalpa for sale. I wanted one, but I was realistic enough to know that on a cabinet-maker's wage I would never be able to afford one, so I had to change direction.

I need to emphasise a point. Back in 1987, when I saw my first ever Lamborghini, I knew that if I worked hard and was disciplined, I would be successful enough to be able to afford one. Not everyone thinks this way. The second time I went to view it I went with a friend by the name of Tommy. His reaction was completely different from mine. When I said that one day I would own a Lamborghini, he laughed and followed his laughter by saying we would never be able to afford a car like that. What Tommy was actually doing was projecting his insecurities and his lack of confidence to be successful onto me. I have experienced this insecure behaviour many times, we can't, we won't, we never will.

Because of their lack of drive and discipline to be successful they try to make themselves feel better by including you. Now ironically Tommy never amounted to anything, ending up on the Great Scrap Heap of life with an ugly wife. Again, I won.

Remember in my introduction the shoe salesmen, both encountered the same situation and their reactions differed from negative to positive? That is exactly what happened the day I slid my ass behind the wheel of that Lamborghini Jalpa and looked at the bull residing at the centre of the steering wheel. That very day when I visualised owning one, I visualised success, Tommy's reaction was one of negativity. Later you will read about the importance of removing negative people from your life.

I visualised having a beautiful home and I have one.

Visualisation is very powerful and will play an integral part in you becoming a Millionaire.

No matter what, never stop VISUALISING – **Write It Down.**

Chapter 5

Cars and Girls

Calculating my wages from cabinet making, my jobs on the side and my making and selling various items I had created out of the firewood offcuts, alongside the two savings accounts I held, which were earning me 8%, as a nineteen-year-old I could be considered as rich.

I made one of the many mistakes in my life which I do not regret as I say, I can win or learn and on this occasion I learned.

I regularly read through the *Autotrader* which, in its day, was the best-selling classified auto magazine, before the paper version was discontinued some years later in favour of the internet. I saw a BMW 320i for sale in Stevenage advertised for £1600, which today would be around £5500 (2024).

I decided I was ready to progress from a £300 Ford Escort Van to a BMW, a very big progression for a nineteen-year-old to make. I had worked hard and believed that one deserved to reward oneself.

I failed to do the research I would conduct today when making a purchase of any kind, and went with the naive approach, that as it was a BMW it must be a sound car. How wrong I was. I went down to Stevenage; everything about this car was wrong but I decided to buy it. BIG mistake. Not too long into my ownership the crankshaft broke, delivering me such a high repair bill that it completely wiped me out. I shall return to that later.

On arriving at work in my new BMW 320i I was greeted with negativity, resentment and jealousy, which was just what I expected of my work colleagues. I was interrogated as to where the cash had come from to make such a purchase. "I saved," was my answer. This did not carry any weight whatsoever as they could not comprehend that the junior cabinet maker earning far less than they were per week could afford such a purchase.

"He must have borrowed the money." "His dad bought it for him." "He got a loan." "He does not own it." Copious amounts of shit came out of their sorry mouths. At no point did any one of them say, "Well done."

Jealousy is a disease worse than cancer. Cancer can be cured, jealousy cannot. You can even smell jealousy, the sufferer stinks of it.

Remember this, throughout your journey to success on your rocky road to becoming a Millionaire, you are going to encounter jealous people. The reason I was able to afford a BMW at the age of 19 and buy it outright with cash was firstly because I was financially astute, and secondly, I had saved. As you are aware I played one building society against the other, seeking out the best place to make my money work for me.

You work hard for your money; your money MUST work hard for you – **Write It Down.**

Now if my work colleagues had been astute enough to stop feeding the till in the many local bars around Nottingham, they too would have built up a much healthier savings pot than I had. They resorted to car finance; you borrow money for a car that, by the time you have made your five years of payments, is worth far less than you originally paid for it and taking into consideration the interest on the loan you are well out of pocket.

So, let's take the figure of £5,000.

You decide to get a loan to purchase a car for that exact figure. By the time you have repaid on the loan in five years' time, your vehicle is only worth, at best, £2000 and your repayments amount to £7000.

That is £5000 wasted that you will never see again; that is me being very generous that your vehicle will be worth £2000 as it may be worth less.

There are exceptions where cars do appreciate in value: my Lamborghini, for example, has increased in value since I first purchased it in 2014, so over the past ten years where most people would lose money on a car, I have made money.

I am going to cover investments in a later chapter, what will and will not make you money.

So back to my BMW. The negativity I received has become a normal part of success; you will have appreciation, and you will have jealousy. In my book *With Confidence* I have a chapter entitled, 'Mixing with the Right Kind of People'. It is vital for your success that you remove negative toxic people from your life NOW!

Successful people think differently, we see opportunities. If we do not see an opportunity, we create one or even several.

So, let's look back. Every Monday morning, I put as much as I could possibly afford into my savings account, the one that rewarded me with the best interest. Along with making things and doing work on the side, I was able to double my income. Now any one of my colleagues could have done the same but they chose not to; life is about choice, you choose how you wish to live your life, how far and how fast you are willing to run.

I will be covering the mindset of a Millionaire in a later chapter. Look back at your work book: remember Attitude Is Everything. I was prepared to run faster and further than any of the colleagues I worked with, because I wanted success.

Going from a £300 Ford Escort Van to a BMW gives people a very different image of you. Now I must stress I do not like stereotypical people who presume just because you drive a £300 van that you are a failure; sadly, people do judge you on how you look, what car you drive, the watch on your wrist. Ironically, I do not have a wristwatch, I am not interested in them, however they are a very good investment, which we will cover later.

So, what happened to my £300 van? I sold it for £300. That van paid for itself many times over and I missed it. A BMW may look the part but try getting eight bags of limestone chippings into one.

On a night out in Nottingham, a friend of a friend met a stripper by the name of Helen. Helen was looking for a driver to take her to the various venues where she worked. Helen was a smart girl and when I say smart, I do not mean her looks. She was attractive, had a great body and knew that her assets could make her wealthy. I was recommended to her as a possible driver. When we met, she thought that my dad owned my BMW, but when she realised that it was mine, and by that I mean, all mine, no finance, she was very impressed.

I was given a trial to take her to a bar in Nottingham where she performed a Strippergram for a man's birthday and after the event she paid me £50 for driving her. It got better; I would regularly drive Helen and a troupe of strippers in my BMW to various venues, earning double my weekly cabinet-making wage in one night.

Then the crankshaft went. This was a seriously expensive job, and the bill completely wiped me out. When I say wiped me out, I mean it put me back into the hundreds as the car also required a new engine. From that day on I referred to them as BM Trouble You's.

It was a very hard lesson and one that I never forgot. I had not done my research, and I paid a hefty price. When I look back, I am so pleased that it happened at such a young age as it set me up to be more aware when making purchases to always do my research.

When making purchases, especially ones of high value, Always Do Your Research – **Write It Down.**

After my BMW was fixed and back on the road, I decided the best move was to sell it and go back to a Ford Escort van. Now my friends and work colleagues found this very amusing, that I had hit the big time and was back down again. As for myself, I looked at the situation very differently. I was not fazed by what anyone thought, whether I did well or not so well. Their reaction towards me was always going to be negative, and also, I live my life for me, NOT for other people's amusement. Fuck Em!

If you have the skills to build a wall and that wall gets destroyed, do you lose the skill to rebuild a better wall? The wall may no longer be there; however, there is always something one can salvage.

Now the way my mind works is as follows:

I will come back stronger and even more successful. I built up wealth once before, I sure can build even greater wealth again, because I am willing to Work Hard and Work Smart.

Tommy, who accompanied me to look at the Lamborghini Jalpa, you remember, the one who was negative about his and also my future success, was an employed flat felt roofer. Tommy had picked up a vast number of jobs on the side and needed a Man with a Van so as to carry out this work at the weekends. Enter Me.

I was introduced to Tommy by a friend through our shared interest in cars. Tommy had a proposition for me. He wanted me to drive across Nottingham from Netherfield, where I worked, on a Friday afternoon and collect bags of limestone chippings from the roofing centre, then on my way home meet him at his place of work and load a bitumen pot into my van. The following Saturday and Sunday mornings I was to be at Tommy's house for 6.30am so that we could tackle the job in question.

For this my reward was £100, which equates to £348 today (2024). For a full week of work at Thomas Pearson I was being paid £75. Who's laughing now?

Alongside helping Tommy, which was most weekends, I was still driving Helen around; yes, she had to settle for a Ford Escort van over a BMW. All credit to the girl, she was prepared to slum it, as she trusted me and I had proven myself to be reliable. Occasionally I would borrow Mum's car, not telling her why, and take Helen and the stripper troupe on various adventures, driving down the road with Mum's words, "Do not have any Jezebel whores in my car" in my mind.

I was banking more money now than ever and hundreds became thousands in my savings accounts. I was the junior cabinet maker earning more in a week than the rest of my colleagues combined. Who's Laughing Now!

As I stated, if you have the ability to build a wall and that wall gets damaged, you may have lost the wall. However, you do not lose the ability to build a more substantial wall. That is exactly how I saw it. I had previously built up a large savings pot and yes, I made the mistake with the BMW and was back at the start; just as in a game of Snakes and Ladders, I progressed up many a ladder and then slid right back down. Yes, my colleagues found this rather amusing, but this did not have any effect on me, as Nothing Ruffles My Feathers. That is exactly how I expect people without ambition to react.

People without ambition end up working for people with ambition – **Write It Down.**

Regardless of what others thought of me, it did not matter, and no way was it going to destabilise my journey to success. I had no issue with driving another £300 Ford Escort van as I knew it would not be forever and because I was always prepared to work hard. I knew no matter what I was destined to become a Millionaire.

Chapter 6

The Hard Way

It was now 1988 and I made one of the best decisions of my life, a decision I had wanted to make for many years, to take up Kung-Fu. It was Monday 11 January 1988 when I telephoned the Nottingham School of Martial Arts to enquire about lessons, and that very night was the beginning of another avenue to great wealth and even greater success.

I must stress a point; I did not initially take up Kung-Fu to make money. My intention was to learn how to fight and fight well. I was astute enough to understand that not only does one need to exercise one's mind, the body requires regular exercise too.

I look for opportunities in everything, that is exactly how entrepreneurs are built. It was at this point that I relinquished my association with Helen, as I was going to dedicate all of my time to Kung-Fu.

Kung-Fu means 'The Hard Way' and I sure was no stranger to hard work. As I have stated and will continue stating, to be successful, to progress to Millionaire status, you MUST be prepared to work hard.

I need you to write this down in your book and onto your vision board. I am prepared no matter what to work hard – **Write It Down.**

It is only going to be through hard work that you will become rich, there are no easy ways.

For those who are fortunate enough to inherit, win, be given, find money, they never keep hold of it for very long. Give a person £1000 and just see how fast they spend it.

If a person works hard and earns £1000, they appreciate and value it more and are wiser with their purchasing decisions. They may choose not to purchase but to invest. The same goes for those who inherit money, it is quickly wasted. There are also those out there who, if they earn £75,000 in one year, always manage to spend £76,000.

Dedication: I would like you to read the dictionary's definition of that very word. That word could very easily sum up my personality. I am dedicated, whatever I set out to do I achieve with great success. As I write this it is September 2024. I am sitting on my sun terrace on what could be called a perfect autumn day, as the temperature would rival any summer's day we have experienced so far this year.

Now through my dedication I have achieved amazing results, and you can too, provided you are prepared to devote a substantial volume of your time to your future success.

To be successful you MUST be Dedicated – **Write It Down.**

I was determined to secure employment during one of the worst recessions this country has ever seen. This was due to being dedicated. When others had set their minds on a future of doom and gloom, I ignored the negativity that surrounded me and worked hard to find a job.

When I enlisted in Shaolin Kung-Fu I was amazed to watch the advanced students performing with such grace and, on those occasions when our class structure consisted of conditioning and destruction, to watch my fellow students break timber and eventually progress to breaking bricks and blocks. This really impressed me, and I wondered if I would ever be able to do that.

Classes were every Monday, Wednesday and Friday, starting at 8.00pm at a cost of £2 per session, which would equate to around £7 today. I was not only investing in my health, I was also investing in my future, as it was Kung-Fu that opened the door to my amazing career as a Stuntman.

My attendance was exemplary. I never missed a class throughout the whole of 1988 and into 1989, because of the very dedication to which I attribute my amazing success; I never give up.

That is one of the qualities you MUST possess to become a Millionaire. Whatever you set your mind to, you MUST be Dedicated. When others stop, make excuses because it is too cold or too hot, or too difficult, or they will start that new venture after they take a vacation – I have heard all the excuses – that is exactly why I would never have a business partner because I know that they would never work as hard as I do.

I attribute this quality to several factors. I was brought up from the age of seven to work, I began paid employment at the age of 16, I have never shied away from hard work. I never make excuses, I DO!

Kung-Fu 'The Hard Way' for a very good reason as anything worth having in life is going to be hard and take Dedication, there is that word again, DEDICATION.

I am super successful because I am Dedicated. Even to this very day I am an Eighth Dan Shaolin Kung-Fu Grandmaster and I will be training as I always do this afternoon and that applies to every weekday afternoon. I train. The only exception is if I am away working as a Stuntman or I am ill.

I embraced every opportunity to train and at Thomas Pearson I cleared a space upstairs in the furniture store so that at lunchtime I could practise my stances.

On a Friday and Saturday evening, when my friends were out getting pissed around the pubs and clubs of Nottingham, I trained. They wasted their money, I invested mine.

You MUST invest not only your money you MUST also invest your time – **Write It Down.**

You must create a plan to structure your week; if you do not already do this you must. The most successful people on this planet are together, they are organised, you need to be too.

In later chapters we will be reviewing various ways to create wealth.

Retention Is Better Than Poor – **Write It Down.**

The meaning of that sentence will become apparent when we review Wealth Creation. Remember this is not a 'Get Rich Quick' read. It is about cultivating a positive mind to take on any venture, handle setbacks and propel you to Millionaire status.

As you have previously read, in my self-help book *With Confidence* there is a chapter entitled, 'Mixing with the Right Kind of People'. During my time at the Nottingham School of Shaolin Kung-Fu I was surrounded by my kind of people. We were all of a similar age, our desire was to progress and be successful in our own right; some of us made it, many sadly failed, simply because they gave up. Every one of the students I trained with, some of whom outranked me, could have done exactly what I did and make a success in the television and movie industry.

Their desire was not as great as mine. Some made it to Red Sash, which is higher than a Black Belt, some failed. Remember, in life it is totally your choice how fast and how far you wish to run.

I chose to run that little bit faster and never stopped. As you will later read, partaking in Kung-Fu changed my life in so many ways and gave me an excellent foundation to becoming a Millionaire.

Chapter 7

Moving On

I was awarded my Shaolin First Dan Red Sash on 12 August 1989, and on that day I met my very first girlfriend. I had dated several girls in the past, but they were never good enough to be promoted from knockoff to serious relationship.

I can give you lots of very positive advice on becoming wealthy, but I must stress when it comes to relationships, BEWARE!

You MUST have a very supportive significant other. I never did, on my travels, and it cost me dearly. It took me until 2020 to find a life partner who was supportive and proud of what I had achieved.

My new girlfriend found it very amusing that she worked 36 hours a week, I worked 40; she was 17 and I was 21, earning £105 per week. As an office clerk she was paid £135. "How are you going to support me on that wage?" I was warned that she was trouble and that she liked to be in control. This was difficult because no one controls me and no one should ever control you, not even our corrupt government (however they do like to try and always fail).

I always have to take a positive from a negative experience and dating Miss Bossy highlighted just how underpaid I was as a craftsman. A friend of mine was delivering pastries, working fewer hours and also earning more than me; his only skill was that he could drive.

When I began my employment at Thomas Pearson in 1984 we were busy, we had a large contract with the East Midlands Electricity Board, which ceased to exist after 1990, and also Prudential Insurance, making all of their office furniture and fitting out every East Midlands Electricity Board shop in the land; a very lucrative contract for a cabinet makers' workshop employing five tradesmen.

The foreman, Dave, who also began at Thomas Pearson when he was just 16, would say to me, "You will be here for life." I worked there for six brilliant years. I have to say that although the salary was poor, I loved every second of working as a cabinet maker; they were some of the best years of my life.

With the added pressure of my then girlfriend highlighting my low earnings and, presuming we had a future together, I was prompted to look for better paid work. It was now 1990 and the man Mum was in a relationship with worked in Leicester as a floor screeder on a building site for Robert McAlpine. He told me that there was a job as a joiner available and I could start as soon as I had worked my notice at Thomas Pearson.

Now back to the negatives: remember when I arrived at work driving my new BMW the reaction I received? Did anyone say, "well done"? No chance, because they were not my kind of people. It was the same when I announced that I would be leaving, the shit began to flow.

'You won't last five minutes on a building site. "You won't leave." "You will be back." What they were really saying was that *they* would not last five minutes on a building site, that *they* would never have the courage to go self-employed and leave what was deemed to be a secure job at Thomas Pearson. Ironically Thomas Pearson closed down in 1995, making the remaining employees redundant.

As well as working as a cabinet maker I had passed my teaching exam and was now a fully qualified Kung-Fu instructor, earning more over two nights than from a full week's cabinet making. So from all the money I had paid out for classes I was now seeing a substantial return.

I left Thomas Pearson in March 1990. I had been there exactly six brilliant years, but it was time to move on. The joinery contract for Robert McAlpine was for three months, and when it came to an end, I decided to set up my own cabinet making and joinery business. With what little money I possessed, I purchased a shed and some machinery and set up my workshop.

In a time when we were suffering another recession, regardless of this the positive was that at the age of 22 I had now escaped 'The Rat Race'. When woodworking was quiet, I would do gardening work and anything that could make me money. I understood the value of being resourceful, I was a hard worker and no matter what was happening in the world it was not going to hold back my journey to becoming a Millionaire.

Times were very tough, in 1990 the country was still in recession and to earn extra cash I decided to offer private Kung-Fu lessons from my home, which allowed me to do my cabinet making and then prepare for my first student of the day.

I am DISCIPLINED, DETERMINED and DEDICATED.

You must be too. To be super successful you MUST be:

DISCIPLINED – **Write It Down.**

DETERMINED – **Write It Down.**

DEDICATED - **Write It Down.**

Everything I have achieved in my life is because I possess those qualities. Without all three you will never be successful, and you WILL NOT become a Millionaire.

Now here is a very interesting episode. The girlfriend at the time made a very big issue of my not earning enough to support her but ironically the very girlfriend and her pathetic mother were now trying to discourage me from starting my own cabinet making and joinery business. They tried to place every form of negativity for starting my own business into my mind and that failed. I looked at their Shit House lives and thought, are you a business mentor? Are you a good ambassador that I need to learn from?

They lived in Shitsville, were in debt, shit shape, shit life, going nowhere fast. I was going to establish my new cabinet making and joinery business no matter what they thought.

Never be put off by negative words of discouragement or you will forever regret not doing what you wanted to do. Use negativity positively and throw even more fuel on your fire of adventure and may it keep burning strong and hot, encouraging you on to even greater goals.

I worked with negative Going Nowhere Fast kind of people as a cabinet maker from 1984 until 1990. I never allowed them to affect me, no matter what. I was going to be successful.

Are you going to walk this earth concerning yourself with what other people think? No, you are not! After reading, absorbing and adapting my words into your life, you are never going to be bothered by what another person says or thinks of you, whether it is positive or negative. They are INSIGNIFICANT.

I was now for the first time in my life an established businessman, self-employed and independent. I have maintained that independence now for the past 34 years. I was no longer a slave to our corrupt government; they were now a slave to me. I would do my cabinet making and joinery by day and teach Kung-Fu by night. Life was hard, work was hard, I was working every possible hour and securing well paid work was very difficult.

Some weeks I would earn nothing in my cabinet making and joinery business, but this did not deter me. I would walk the streets, putting my business card and leaflets through people's doors to generate work; wherever there was a noticeboard in a DIY shop I would attach my business card to it.

I learned from a very early age that you MUST Make It Happen! – **Write It Down.**

The 1990 recession had a detrimental effect on trade resulting in my business suffering financially. My earnings were so low that my then girlfriend came to the conclusion that she could do better and that I was not rich enough; she yearned for a rich guy. She left me in the autumn of that year. She actually did me a big favour as she was draining and negative.

Ironically this very girlfriend contacted me 20 years later, informing me just how amazing I was and that she had known I would make it and asking if I would like to meet up. Interesting that when I did not have a Pot To Piss In she did not want to know me.

I struggled on; life was very hard, however I never give up, as I never expect life to always be easy. Remember diamonds are formed under extreme pressure.

Be a Diamond – **Write It Down.**

Looking at my weekly income from my cabinet making and joinery business, I was able to establish that for all the very hard work I was putting in, my return from teaching Kung-Fu was much greater. I worked fewer hours as a Kung-Fu instructor and earned more money. At this stage in my life even though I was ambitious I did not know that Kung-Fu was going to make me very rich.

It was now 1991 and I was due to travel to Hanover, Germany, to take my Second Dan. It was a journey that completely changed my way of thinking.

Chapter 8

Know Your Worth

While at my school in Hanover, after passing my Second Dan, I observed the German students' fascination with Kung-Fu films. There was a viewing room where, after training, one could relax and watch movies, the movies of choice being martial arts films, from Bruce Lee to the more modern Hollywood-produced shite.

I sat at the back, analysing; what I was able to establish was that the martial arts actors were no better nor worse than I. Therefore, when the German students dreamed of being a martial arts actor, I thought differently; I was *going* to be a martial arts actor, I was going to Make It Happen!

I decided to return to England and enrol in drama classes.

I will take this very opportunity to stress a point; many people in life will moan and complain about their current financial situation and do absolutely nothing about it.

I am resourceful. I am inventive, creative, sharp, together, talented and more than anything I am capable. The most successful people in the world have these qualities. These are not qualities one is born with; they are qualities one develops, life skills necessary to becoming super successful and a Millionaire.

You can exhaust your energy by complaining about how life dealt you an unfair hand, or you can be resourceful and do something about it. Remember what you last wrote in your book:

Be A Diamond and Make It Happen.

If we wind right back to my Youth Training Scheme days, I was motivated enough then to improve my situation; then look at the day I witnessed the red Ferrari and the white Porsche 911 Cabriolet, again motivating me to work hard, seeking out opportunities to become wealthy and super successful, as I wanted that life.

Whatever I decide to do in life, I do my research. So here I was, seeking out a reputable drama school in Nottingham to take acting lessons to make myself even more marketable.

You have to spend money to make money – **Write It Down.**

My desire was to break into the television and film industry as a martial arts actor, so I required an acting qualification and an Equity card.

I was working at cabinet making and joinery by day, coupled with teaching Kung-Fu and then attending drama classes one evening per week with the occasional private lesson. My drama teacher made it very clear that there was no way possible that I could work in the very lucrative television and film industry without an Equity card. I had heard of such an item; however, I had no real understanding what one was – it was union membership and without this I could not work.

I will take this opportunity to stress that I am no longer a member of Equity because of their pathetic left-wing W.O.K.E. agenda, which has totally ruined our industry. One does not even need an Equity card any longer to work in film and television, so it is now seen as a complete waste of money paying into a union that does not have any power and is ridiculed throughout the industry.

So, another hurdle was placed in my path. Now to be successful in life you must only see these events as temporary; they can be overcome. It was not impossible to obtain an Equity card but hard work was required yet again, something I was used to.

I did not receive any support whatsoever in obtaining union membership. I must say my drama teacher was very negative towards my entering into a world I knew absolutely nothing about and offered no help and advice as to how I could achieve what I now required.

Being resourceful I ask lots of questions, I am interested, I like to know. So, to go back to when I was training at my first Kung-Fu school in Nottingham, during a conversation I had with one of my fellow students I discovered that by night he was a club singer.

I gave him a call and arranged a meeting, told him about my situation and asked if he could help me. Entertainers were entitled to apply to Equity for union membership; it was not required in order to be a club singer, but it gave them some protection if a venue refused to pay them, as Equity would take up the cause. Now again I was laughed at and also told that I would never make it. Never be afraid to ask for help despite what others may think of you.

I found that in life I had a good ability to make positive decisions, despite the way others were trying to influence me. If anyone puts me down or tries to knock me back it makes me more determined to achieve my goal and prove them wrong.

My colleagues and friends suffered with very negative personalities; their ethics clashed with mine on so many subjects, as from a very young age I developed a 'Do It' attitude, meaning that if I wanted to achieve something I would Do It, to the constant ridicule of many individuals. As we know, people who try and knock you back are very insecure about their own abilities in life and are frightened to stand out and be different.

It was agreed that after taking singing lessons I would accompany my friend to various venues around the midlands to perform. His reward for helping me was that I taught him Kung-Fu, deal done. In life there will be times when you can trade your time using your skills and knowledge, it is very much how the bartering system first started before money ever changed hands.

I have a certain skill and that skill could help another who in turn could help me with his expertise. Today money has replaced bartering in most aspects of modern life.

I worked on a Country and Western routine, with some Eagles tracks, which were always well received no matter what age the audience was. I also threw in The Drifters and a Hermans Hermits song, 'Years May Come, Years May Go' which Mum used to play on a Sunday while she was preparing our lunch after we had returned from Mass.

I remembered so much of the song, and enjoyed singing it, so I decided to include it in my set. After many months of performing on stage, each booking bringing me even closer to my goal of obtaining my Equity card, I eventually received it in September of that year. Ironically today you can get an Equity card very easily, and you do not even have to work to obtain what was once nearly impossible but well deserved, making Equity membership totally pointless and a waste of money in today's entertainment world. In fact, you are much better off without one.

I continued at drama school, earning a distinction, a qualification that would be a great asset to my stunt work, leaving my club singing days behind so that I could concentrate on making it into film and television. When I succeeded, I visited the so-called friend who had helped me, receiving only negativity from him, saying I would never work. At the time of my visit, I had already worked on over 30 productions. I never saw him again.

You MUST remove all negativity from your life, keep your association with negative people to an absolute minimum. If you have not already done so, purchase, read and absorb my book *With Confidence* and read 'Mixing with the Right Kind of People'. It will really help you on your journey to success.

I found that my drama school was unhelpful in steering me in the right direction to make it as a martial arts actor, so again it was down to my determined attitude to make this happen. So here I was with a Second Dan in Shaolin Kung-Fu, a drama qualification and most of all the Equity card everyone said I would need; and where was the work? I got back on the telephone to sell myself, but the problem was no one really knew how to guide me.

A chance telephone call to Equity, the actors' union, brought me the answer I needed, in a conversation that would change my life. The staff member I was talking to was John Barclay, a very helpful person who listened to my story of hard work obtaining my Equity card coupled with drama and Kung-Fu. John's reply was, "Have you thought about becoming a Stuntman?" I was amazed by this as I thought one had to be born into that kind of work. John explained what was required and that the stunt register was managed by Equity, posted me out the criteria, and I was now on my very hard journey to becoming a Stuntman!

Chapter 9

You Have To Make It Happen

Now absolutely nothing worth having in life comes to you easily. You, and only you, have to make it happen.

I have to make it happen – **Write It Down.**

Also put those words on your Vision Board too.

Now what I require you to do every day is observe your vision board, look at what you have embellished it with and what affirmations are written there. As I write this in my study looking out onto my driveway at my amazing Lamborghini, I have my vision board in front of me. Even today with my Millionaire status and super success I still utilise the benefits of my vision board because it has never failed me since I introduced it into my life as far back as the 1980s.

Now here is a very interesting point; even before I knew what a vision board was, I had already created one. That is exactly how my mind works. Coupled with visualisation, I visualised success, I visualised being super successful and wealth naturally followed.

So, when others were focusing on negativity and negative events were constantly happening to them, my energy was always focused in a positive direction and on what I needed to do To Make It Happen.

Look at what you have achieved so far in your life, all the products that you made happen; I am sure there are more than you realise. Learning to drive, if you cannot yet drive you may now be researching, learning your theory and visualising the freedom and employment opportunities driving affords you.

When I look back at my achievements and putting the time into writing this book, I can clearly see at each stage of my life I did exactly what it took to progress, no excuses, no moaning, no complaining, I got on with it, I worked hard, prised my ass out of bed and **Made It Happen** and that is exactly what you are also going to do.

So you want to be rich, you would like to be a Millionaire, what about a Billionaire, it is possible, we will be covering wealth creation in a later chapter. This is the perfect time to

Make Your Plan!

When the telephone rings and I am contracted to undertake a stunt job, I have a list that I take out of my study drawer comprising everything I need to take with me. I created this list when I first became a Stuntman back in 1993 and as time and experience went on the list became bigger, as I acquired more equipment to make 'Falling for You' even more marketable.

As you are aware, I am super organised, everything has its place, and I never lose anything. My organisation skills are simply the best, they have to be because if I spent time trying to find a folder containing important documents that is time wasted that could have been utilised to create even more wealth.

I simply love money.

Time for you to break off reading and now go and make your plan, what exactly do YOU wish to achieve? Remember this book is about you, yes you are reading my long hard journey to success so you can input all the vital skills into your venture. However, I am there, I am successful, super successful, now it is your turn.

Pen Pencil and Paper Time, write down what you would like to achieve, what it will take and how you are **Going To Make It Happen.** Have you already got the images on your vision board? If not, why not? Everything in life begins with a vision.

Whatever you desire, be prepared to be laughed at, it is going to happen. When I decided I wanted to be a Stuntman many of my friends laughed at me, and very few thought I would ever make it. Some so-called friends even tried to put me off by attempting to fill my mind with negative thoughts. Every person who said I would not succeed gave me so much more drive and energy to achieve my goal and prove them wrong. My dream of becoming a Stuntman was very difficult but realistic; I was physically fit, enthusiastic and most of all through my Kung-Fu training, dedicated and confident enough to believe in myself and I was prepared for hard work.

You only have to look at my stunt website to see how much I have achieved. You too will achieve as much or as little as you would like, but remember it is down to you and only you to make it happen.

When I have conversations with people about money and success and what they would like to achieve, a common reply is, "I don't have the money to achieve what I would really like."

Now later you will read just how expensive training to become a Stuntman was and how I overcame this financial obstacle. There is always a way; remember what I said in the introduction to my book: Hard Work. To save you the time of looking back here are those very words again:

I MUST stress you will have to WORK HARD. Nothing worth having in life comes to us that easily, you MUST be prepared to WORK HARD, if not you WILL FAIL.

Lazy Bastards need not apply.

If you are lazy and make pathetic excuses like it's cold, it's raining, I will do it tomorrow, I am tired, I have a stomach ache, I will do it on my day off; forget it, you have already failed, and you DO NOT have what it takes to become a Millionaire.

Successful people do not make excuses, they do no matter how they feel, no matter what the weather, **They Make It Happen.**

I have lost count of how many excuses I have heard from people through the years, they never progressed, became wealthy and super successful and now they have another excuse to add to their very long list, however they are far too stupid to acknowledge that they are their own worst enemy and the real truth is they are lazy, simple as.

And do not ever tell me you do not have time, come spend some time with me and see just how much I achieve in 24 hours. If you claim you do not have enough time, prise your ass out of your warm bed an hour earlier five days a week, which would equate to 20 hours in just one month, now tell me you do not have the time.

You MUST believe in yourself, if you do not believe in yourself, how can you expect anyone else to believe in you?

If you are a lazy person you will fail, no matter what you do you will fail. If you are not prepared for hard work forget reading any further, if you are the type of person who expects everything to fall from the sky and this perfect life form around you, you have already failed, life just does not happen that way.

Even writing this chapter of my book today, I broke off to do two hours of training; I also have to manage my stunt company, 'Falling For You', and I have to manage my personal development business, 'The Strategist', as well as other commitments throughout my day. I do all of this no matter what and I am a self-made Millionaire.

I could retire right now, plonk my ass down on a beach and observe the sunset; would that make me happy? For a time, possibly. Would I be satisfied? For a time, I would. Would that suit my lifestyle? For a week, at the most. I love working, I love being productive, I love to help people who appreciate my help and most of all I simply love making money.

I work hard 365 days a year and if you yearn to be super successful and a Millionaire you will need to as well. **No Excuses.**

Now write out your plan of how you are going to Make It Happen.

Chapter 10

Disciplined – Determined – Dedicated

It was January 1992 when John Barclay sent me the criteria to become an Equity registered Stuntman. Now I will take this opportunity to inform you that the Equity stunt register was formed in 1973 and sadly was dissolved in September 2017. It no longer exists; it is now, sadly, The Wild West out there with the stunt world left unregulated.

If someone was venturing into the world of stunts today, they would never make a living, as there are those out there who are willing to work for as little as £50 a day or worse, sell their sorry ass for free. Just to put those figures into context, my daily rate as a Stuntman is in the thousands and I demand royalties too.

The final destroyer of the film and television industry will be Artificial Intelligence. Nothing intelligent about it whatsoever, it WILL destroy the stunt industry and sadly stunt professionals will be no longer required, surplus to requirement.

When I absorbed what was required, what became apparent to me was that this would not be easy. In fact, to become an Equity-registered Stuntman was by far the toughest training of any occupation on Earth and that is no exaggeration, it is not easy and rightfully so. Stunt work is one of the most dangerous occupations in the world and, having been regularly working in the industry since 1993 I now know why the criteria were set so high.

The training, commonly referred to as 'Disciplines', was broken down into sections:

Fighting

Falling

Riding and Driving

Agility and Strength

Water

Miscellaneous

What one required was six disciplines from a list of 13 skills relevant to stunt work, falling into a minimum of four categories; the fighting category was compulsory.

In the fighting category alongside Karate, Judo, Wrestling and Boxing was Kung-Fu. One was required to be brown sash or higher; as I had just been awarded my Second Dan I required five more skills.

I chose Trampolining from the falling category, Horse Riding from the Riding and Driving category, Gymnastics from the Agility and Strength category, Swimming from the Water category, Hang Gliding from the Miscellaneous category. I chose to also train in Fencing and SCUBA Diving, progressing to the qualification of Rescue Diver. I knew that having these additional skills would be a great asset to my career as a Stuntman.

Who's laughing now. I have that very saying written on a photograph I have on my study wall, of me standing next to my Lamborghini, displaying my impressive £50,000 RIKY X registration plate.

Yes, you guessed it, when I announced that I was training to become a Stuntman the negativity began to flow. The usual shite such as 'You won't do it', 'You will never get any work.' Now there I was, a Second Dan Shaolin Kung-Fu expert, which takes a massive amount of hard work and dedication, and I was being challenged yet again. Now as you are patently aware, when certain individuals have the audacity to doubt you, it is a reflection of their own insecurity and lack of confidence. They would love to have the courage to do exactly what you intend to do.

Fuel for My Fire always kicks in when these situations occur.

One of the most difficult obstacles I encountered was getting some of the instructors to return my calls. I was amazed at just how slack they were, despite paying them well for their services. Nothing has changed in all the years, in fact people's unreliable nature today is disgraceful and then they moan and complain that life never goes their way.

I am relentless. As my gymnastics instructor failed to return any of my calls, I visited his office and waited there from 9.00am until at 5.30pm he walked through the door, providing me with an apology for not communicating. Basically, he could not be bothered. If he had been he would have returned one of my many telephone calls. Ironically, one of his friends was a Stuntman, and he was very well aware of what was required to, as he called it, 'work towards your stunt ticket.' I did not take his unprofessional attitude personally. I never get emotional in these situations; I needed a qualification and for a time I needed him to teach and grade me. He was a very good gymnastics instructor and a very bad businessman. We struck a very fair deal and the following Wednesday I began my course.

Not all instructors were unreliable; my horse riding instructor was very good, offering me free riding lessons if I worked at the riding school, an offer which I accepted, allowing me to learn to ride for free and only paying for private tuition when required. I was cantering on my first riding lesson. I had never ridden a horse before, my instructor said she had never in all her years known a pupil to take to riding a horse as easily as I had. I credit that ability to my Kung-Fu, which develops great balance, posture, strength and control.

I was jumping on my third lesson. My instructor worked on the finer details of the skills I needed to achieve to pass my Stunt Register Horse Riding Test, which was held at a riding school arranged by Equity and supervised by a horse master from the Stunt Register. A British Horse Society riding instructor was also present to adjudicate.

Once I had all the instructors in place, I designed a timetable allowing me to maximise my time, something even to this day I still adopt in my life. I am a very organised person with military precision. Motivating myself has never been a problem. I found all my training very enjoyable as it introduced me to new skills that I would never have been interested in if it had not been for my stunt training.

Funding my training was somewhat problematic at times, as not only is one having to pay instructors but also purchase clothing and equipment for the chosen disciplines, as well as fuelling a vehicle, in my case my £300 Ford Escort van, which to its credit travelled all over the country, allowing me to complete my training.

The first few weeks were the most difficult, as my body had to adapt to so many different skills in a short space of time. As anyone will tell you who has completed training, to gain acceptance onto the (then) stunt register you acquire many injuries along the way, which can slow your progress down considerably.

As time went on everything started to fall into place with my training routine. I would not say it became any easier, but my body and mind began to adjust to what I was putting it through on a daily basis. I soon discovered with my training that it did not matter how fit one was but that until you learned the techniques of each chosen discipline, fitness did not matter. I am a quick learner whatever I choose to do and coupled with dedication I worked hard to develop the standard required. My life became eating, sleeping, training and working whenever possible to earn money to fund my disciplines.

For that year I did nothing else, I did not socialise, I did not see friends or family, I just dedicated myself to training to obtain my goal. Remember what you read in previous chapters about **Hard Work,** nothing in life worth having will come to you easily, you have to work hard and that is exactly what I did.

The first certificate I was awarded was in gymnastics, a very difficult qualification to pass. My Wednesday afternoons consisted of travelling to a local leisure center in Nottingham to train with a small group of gymnasts under a retired Olympic gymnastics instructor. I now required only four more skills and I would be there. My gymnastics instructor allowed me to use the facilities as much as I wanted for free, an offer I accepted as the gym was fitted with a sunken trampoline surrounded by crash mats allowing me to practise my trampolining as much as I wished.

Any free time I had, I went to the leisure centre and put in as many hours as possible on the trampoline and also practised my gymnastics. It was some months later that I passed my swimming qualification. For this, training consisted of being in the pool at 7.00am five mornings a week at an old Victorian swimming pool, which was cockroach infested. Whatever it took I was there, no excuses that the water was cold, no excuses that it was an icy winter's morning, no excuses, I trained.

I was delighted when I accomplished my swimming qualification as the swimming pool was disgusting and should have been condemned. As it was owned by Nottingham City Council there was no chance of that happening as the (then) council would have happily had members of the public swimming around in rats' piss as long as they were making money; in fact, we probably were.

Only three disciplines left to go. It was now January 1993 and along with my swimming I had now passed my trampolining exam, which was one of the most difficult to do. I had hired a trampoline with an instructor and dedicated several evenings in the week to trampolining. I met some great people who became good friends.

Now that I had completed my swimming exam and passed trampolining, it freed up my mornings to leave early to go hang gliding. This qualification was later removed from the list as it could be completed from novice to pilot in two weeks, weather permitting. In England it was very rare that one was able to complete the course within this time, as on average it took pupils around three months. It was such an enjoyable experience, soaring over the Derbyshire countryside above Ashbourne.

Disciplined – Determined – Dedicated

The High Peaks of Derbyshire have amazing views and very unpredictable weather, which we experienced in several training sessions.

Whatever qualification I was working on at the time, scraping the ice from my van on a winter's morning made me even more determined to achieve my goal. The long drives to reach several of my destinations, the expense of travelling, all made me determined to see it through. I could not afford accommodation in Ashbourne, so I slept in the back of my van overnight.

Training to become a Stuntman is not just about gaining six disciplines, it conditions your body and mind for the tough world of stunt work, as if one is not prepared for the travelling, the unexpected cancellations due to adverse weather conditions, and training in a very cold environment, then one is definitely not cut out to be a Stuntman.

Just to put this into perspective, when the stunt register existed Equity would receive around 10,000 enquiries a year and out of those only six applicants would gain acceptance on to the stunt register. That demonstrates just how difficult it was to become a Stuntman.

I had a truly professional and highly skilled hang gliding instructor and by March I had qualified. I was just waiting for Equity to inform me when they were holding the next riding test. The date for this came through in April. Just one more exam to go and I would have achieved the six disciplines required to gain access to the (then) stunt register. I was listed onto the riding test which was held at a riding school near Epping Forest in Essex.

On that day I met other people who were training for the (then) stunt register too. It was interesting to speak to likeminded people who were the same age as I, already had a background of working in a variety of occupations and, like me, had then decided to train to become a Stuntman.

It was a difficult test, having to not only prove one's ability to tack a horse up then ride it to British Horse Society standards, but also to ride with restricted vision wearing a jousting helmet and carrying a sword and accomplishing the various sections of the test on three horses all with different temperaments. I now understand, after doing several stunts with horses, why the test had to be so strict. I was very pleased to be informed that I had passed. It was an amazing feeling to think that in just over a year of training I had achieved my goal. Not only had I passed my horse-riding test, I now possessed all six certificates to gain entrance to the (then) stunt register.

The Stunt Committee met on Sunday 18th of April 1993. This was back then referred to as a Membership Meeting where the day was spent looking through applications from individuals who wished to join the stunt register and to look at Probationary and Intermediate members who wished to be promoted through the ranks.

All I required now was for the Equity Executive Committee to endorse the Stunt Committee's decision to accept me onto the stunt register. I would then have achieved my goal of becoming a Stuntman. This was completed at the Equity Office on Tuesday 20th April 1993. I had been successful; I was now a Stuntman.

What a feeling after all the hard work and training! Here I was, joining an elite group of individuals in the amazing world of television and film stunt work. I remember that conversation so well, I stood in my lounge in Rise Park taking the call.

That very conversation with Equity staff member John Barclay, back in January 1992, changed my life. I always tell people that it was I who made that change, firstly by deciding that it was my desire to become a Stuntman then by putting in the hours and very hard work that was required to achieve this. Nothing to do with luck; I do not believe in luck anyway, nothing to do with being in the right place at the right time. It was down to my making a decision, conducting my research and accomplishing exactly what I had set out to do.

The reason I tell you this story is because you MUST **Make It Happen.** It will not come to you, you need to be so hungry that no matter what,

Disciplined – Determined – Dedicated

nothing is going to stop you achieving your goal and many amazing goals after that, again through HARD WORK.

Now that I was a member of the (then) British Equity Stunt Register I had to be patient and wait for the telephone to ring. This is where most people fall down in life, they do not have the patience that life sometimes requires.

I was told by the secretary of the British Equity Stunt Register of many a new member who lacked the discipline that the film and television industry required, losing patience and telephoning Stunt Co-ordinators begging for work, then becoming a nuisance and making themselves unemployable.

I learned several valuable lessons from Kung-Fu, one of which was to have great patience in life, a quality I possess which has always paid off for me. This quality is vital to survive in such a volatile industry. It was not too long before my patience paid off and the telephone was ringing with my first job.

Chapter 11

Residual Income

Now this is a very good moment to explain to you that despite wanting a much better and more rewarding life, I did not become a Stuntman for the money. I had no idea how much a Stuntman earned and even to this very day I feel Stuntmen are underpaid and undervalued. That is for two reasons, **Supply** and **Demand.** We will talk more about **Supply** and **Demand** in a later chapter.

So, my friends had written me off and there was I, now a television and film Stuntman, how cool was that. My first job was on the BBC television series *Casualty*, which was on my 26th birthday in August 1993. What an amazing day that was. It was shot in Bristol. I was now for the first time in my life experiencing show business.

Back when the stunt register existed, one was accepted as a probationary member, which meant being supervised by a fully qualified Stunt Co-ordinator for a minimum of three years. During that time, in order to be promoted to Intermediate member one had to have worked for 60 days and performed a minimum of 36 identified stunts.

Now that may sound easy, but believe me, when I qualified there were many probationary members who had stagnated for the past ten years and still had not achieved the required stunts to meet the criteria for promotion. A Stuntman is self-employed so if there is no work there is little possibility of progress.

I was very fortunate that, due to being only 5 feet 3 inches in stature, I carved a niche out for myself as a child and teenage stunt double, and also playing teenagers. When I applied for my promotion to Intermediate member I had accumulated over 300 days' work and over 70 identifiable stunts. With common sense and by being astute I observed other Stuntmen, and what equipment they carried, and invested in everything I would need to be successful.

I also learned how to handle a powerboat, bought an off-road enduro motorbike and every available Friday would ride in Clipstone, an area of Mansfield known as 'The Desert', to perfect my skills.

At every available opportunity I trained, whether that meant taking an old car to a disused airfield and skidding it around, or free climbing and abseiling, or purchasing a quantity of cardboard boxes to practise high and low falls, or practising with fire, which became one of my specialties.

Being fiercely ambitious, my sights were firmly set on becoming a Stunt Co-ordinator, as that would make me even more employable. Again I worked and trained hard, kept myself in peak physical fitness and also progressed with my Kung-Fu, to which I owe my amazing life and career.

I made myself immensely employable.

Now as an Intermediate member I was able to promote myself on a world-wide scale. As a solo Stuntman, an Intermediate member was not allowed to Co-ordinate until they had worked in the role for a minimum of two years and had worked for 24 separate film and television companies, all on Equity contracts. The Equity contract was vital for the following reasons.

What I was totally unaware of was something called royalties, so that when my episode of *Casualty* was repeated I received 80% of my original fee. When my episode is put onto VHS or DVD, I also receive a royalty fee; when my episode is sold abroad, again I receive a percentage of my fee. ITV has a similar system, paying out 55% of one's repeat fee. So as a new Stuntman not only was I earning income from the actual stunts I was regularly performing, I was earning money while I slept, from residual income.

To become wealthy, you need to create for yourself Residual Income – **Write It Down.**

The royalty system applied to television only and not feature films. For myself, even though I did work on Hollywood movies, I much preferred television work as it was more lucrative.

So, when I became an Intermediate Stuntman I did something that was frowned upon by my colleagues, I promoted myself. By that I mean I had business cards and brochures printed and a showreel produced; I established my company 'Falling For You' on an international scale.

I looked at my career this way. I was self-employed, so if I were a self-employed plumber would I not promote myself to obtain work and build up a customer base? I sure would, so why should being a Stuntman be any different?

What I established was that some of my colleagues were insecure and did not have the courage to break away from the regular 'cliquey' groups they were working in. For myself, being fiercely ambitious, I saw my career in a completely different light.

So, what if I had decided just to rely on a steady flow of work from certain Stunt Co-ordinators? This works for a time; however, there are several factors that can change the dynamics at any chosen moment, including death, ill health and retirement. At any point, any one or all of the said Stunt Co-ordinators could leave the industry and leave me without my steady flow of work.

I am far more intelligent and forward thinking than most people. I look at all eventualities and I prepare, remember the Cub Scout motto **Be Prepared.** You even have it written in your book.

My focus was on being in the strongest and most employable position possible, hence promoting myself to production companies, and it paid off. Posting out 250 of my 'Falling For You' brochures created an abundance of work, so not only was I receiving work from the regular

Stunt Co-ordinators I had worked for as a probationary Stuntman, I was now also receiving additional work directly from production companies, allowing me for the first time in my career to set my own daily rate.

What I did was unheard of in the stunt world. I put my rates right up for the following reasons.

Firstly, I always believed that Stuntmen were underpaid and undervalued.

Secondly, if my daily rate was the same as that of every other Intermediate Stuntman I would not stand out, so I set a very high daily rate, and today I am one of the most expensive Stuntmen you can book, reassuringly expensive, I always say.

What you have to do is Know Your Worth – **Write It Down.**

You must never be afraid to charge a high fee for your services.

Thirdly, I love money.

Now the jealousy, envy and resentment started, yes that incurable disease, JEALOUSY yet again recurring. Nothing ruffles my feathers, as experiencing individuals being resentful towards me has no effect whatsoever, it is just how I expect certain individuals to be anyway, so I am never surprised when it happens.

What you have to be aware of and prepared for on your long hard road to success is people without talent or ambition putting you down. Let them get on with it. Keep your association with toxic people to an absolute minimum.

Not only was I receiving a regular income from my stunt work, I was also receiving substantial royalty payments.

You must create for yourself multiple income streams – **Write It Down.**

We will explore income streams in a later chapter, for now think about what talents you currently hold that can earn you an income.

Brochures and showreel sent out = work flowing in. I was living the dream, having the Best Job in the Whole Wide World.

Chapter 12

Money Makes Money

1994 was my first full year as a Stuntman. I was still working as a cabinet maker and joiner between stunt engagements. Work was now regular and there just did not seem any point in doing woodwork jobs when I was earning around five hundred pounds a day as a Stuntman; my free time was better spent training and promoting my business. I sold my workshop and some machinery in 1997 when I moved out of the family home.

I was collecting the required 24 days to become a Stunt Co-ordinator. This in its day was very difficult, as one had to work as a solo Stuntman on several jobs for several different production companies where no other stunt professionals were present and one was not allowed to Co-ordinate. Falling downstairs, skidding cars around, jumping a motorbike off a ramp into the sea or even stunt doubling for Ronnie Corbett on a Pizza Hut commercial were qualifying days.

Now the clever bit. As you are aware, from a very young age I saved; I considered it a very good habit to possess. I was smart enough to realise that if I wanted great wealth and to become a Millionaire, I needed to make my money work for me.

I have worked hard for my money; my money now has to work hard for me!

Write It Down.

I had set myself a target that for each year of working as a Stuntman I would try and save £10,000 in the highest interest account I could find. I also invested in five- and ten-year bonds. Now interest rates have been shockingly low for several years, controlled by our corrupt government, more about that in a later chapter.

So, after 10 years of saving, I would have £100,000 plus all the interest my investments had accumulated.

Money Makes Money – **Write It Down.**

So now my money was working hard for me.

If you would rather piss money down the pub, you won't get rich.

If you would rather spend your money on pointless holidays, you won't get rich.

If you would rather squander your money on fags and booze, you won't get rich.

If you would rather waste your money on Netflix and Spotify subscriptions, you won't get rich.

If you would rather splurge your money on takeaways, you won't get rich.

If you would rather throw away your money on shitty festivals, you won't get rich.

If you would rather deplete your money by covering your body with tramp stamps, you won't get rich.

If you would rather blow your money on the 3.30 at Haydock Park, you won't get rich.

Those individuals who strive to become Millionaires never waste their money.

I see this so many times, people going to work each day, stopping off to purchase their lunch, too fucking lazy to even get themselves their breakfast, they buy that too, instead of being organised and going to the grocery store and purchasing what they need for the week, putting some effort in and making their lunch at home the night before.

When I was a cabinet maker, Roy, Andy and Miserable Nev all complained on a near-daily basis of not having enough money, yet they never brought in lunch. It was my job to go to the shops and pick it up for them. They never had a problem getting their ass to the local boozer to get pissed out of their faces each evening, yet did not have the time or knowhow to make their lunch for the following day.

Now your lifestyle choices are purely yours, when you have made your first million and you desire said rewards you have every right to be lavish, however you are not there yet and believe me, every penny counts and even when you achieve Millionaire status they still do.

The best bit was that some years I was able to invest more than the £10,000 target I had set myself and do you know why? Because I was prepared to make sacrifices, no pointless holidays, not wasting time and money down the pub, no needless subscriptions, no gambling, it all adds up.

I now want you to look at all the subscriptions you are contracted to. Write them all down with the annual figures that each and every one is costing you, total that figured up and ask yourself, do I really need all of this shit? Time wasted on watching Netflix is time you could be investing in making money.

Time spent shopping on Amazon is time and money wasted, remember what I said in Chapter Three, <u>Purchase only what you need NOT what you want.</u>

It truly amazes me just how many people have no real knowledge of their weekly, monthly and yearly spend, using Direct Debit for everything, which results in them becoming clueless on their finances.
You MUST know where every penny you earn goes.

Now you have written down your list of subscriptions, look at the cost, review your usage and ask yourself, am I working towards making myself rich or making myself poor and another man rich?

Those subscriptions need to go.

Now I do not and have never used Direct Debit. The reason this form of payment was created in the first place was because most people are so forgetful that they do not even have the social intelligence to know when to pay their household bills.

Also, because most people never check their bank statements, more money than was necessary could be taken from one's account and those that are as Thick As Pig Shit would never realise.

You do not need to be using Direct Debit for anything. Every bill you have you can pay by cash or by debit card at a time of your choosing.

Here is a fine example. I receive my electricity bills one each month; on the first of the month I provide my supplier with a meter reading, they then provide me with a bill, which I then pay by cash. What could be more simple?

It astounds me when I hear that most people do not do this, receiving an aggregated bill. Working in this fashion, they allow their energy company to take more money than is required and have some pay their bill and the rest sit there in credit one would hope to cover the next bill.

I ask you this question, would you pole up to a filling station in your Lamborghini and put more cash over the counter than is necessary so that on your next visit you were in credit?

Would you Fuck!

Would you go to the supermarket till and give an extra £130 over the counter to cover your next visit?

Would you Fuck!

So why are you doing that with your energy supplier?

From today, cancel all Direct Debits, pay your utility bill only with cash and only when the bill comes in and pay only what you owe.

The next thing you must do is have a paper bank statement sent to you through the post, this is an absolute must, fuck all this saving the planet shite, that Will Not make you rich.

This is about YOU!

When that bank statement arrives, you are going to scrutinise it, and I mean scrutinise. You are going to check every transaction so that you know exactly where your money is going. You are going to use cash, pound notes, at every available opportunity, and if you encounter a company that has a sign saying, 'Card Payments Only', walk away.

I do this all the time. **Cash Is King** and in a later chapter you will read why.

Most people are brainwashed into doing what the government needs them to do – the Sheeple of life. To be super successful, to become a Millionaire or even a Billionaire you have to think and act differently and that is exactly what I do.

Chapter 13

Picks and Shovels

I never wanted a mortgage. I knew that having one went against my principle of being in control. It is impossible to control me as I have created my very own set of rules adopted to my life, I do not obey the law, why should I, the law is a complete farce, again controlled by our incredibly corrupt government.

I knew that through hard work it would be possible to never borrow money. Most people do not think this way because they are not patient and yearn to live a lavish lifestyle; you can, when you are a self-made Millionaire, live whatever lifestyle you choose.

From 1993 to 1999 interest rates were fluctuating between five and seven percent, which is nothing. Even though interest rates were very low I still saved and invested what money I had.

I left the family home in 1997 and lodged at a friend's parents' house, this again was no great inconvenience as I never stayed a full week there in the year and a half of my residence as I was always away working. I had a fascination with cars, supercars, that is, Lamborghinis and Ferraris, and would regularly monitor the market and establish which cars were going to be the best investments.

Now at this stage in my life I did not possess a home, however I was actively saving. Remember the £10,000 per year I was putting away. By 1997 I had managed to save around £60,000, which today would equate to £133,000.

Property prices were still high and even though £60,000 was a pretty impressive sum of money to hold, it was not going to buy me a decent house outright.

Back in 1800s America a gold rush was taking place; the discovery led to thousands of prospectors rushing to dig for their fortune. Now here is the clever bit, those prospectors needed tools, picks and shovels, also substantial clothing. If one was to set up a shop selling such vital equipment, one would not even need to go into the mines; one would have one's very own gold mine, making oneself much richer than the very people who were purchasing one's products.

Levi Strauss saw an opportunity during the American gold rush and created his famous denim jeans, which were then sold to gold prospectors who required heavy duty work pants for all that a-diggin' that was to be a done.

So, when I invest, I adopt the Picks and Shovels approach.

There is money to be made from everything – **Write It Down.**

I see an opportunity in everything. You have to seek out those opportunities, they are all around you. In 1999 health and safety was becoming very prominent in industry and I noticed an opportunity that very few of my colleagues saw. Companies were required to have made a twenty-minute safety video that they could show to their staff during an induction, to make them aware of workplace hazards and dangers. These videos were created by what was referred to as the non-broadcast video market. I looked at where these companies advertised their services and I, too, advertised mine, coupled with which I picked up the telephone and called them. This was before email had come into public existence, and it secured me some very lucrative work, even doing an all-terrain-vehicle safety video for none other than the Health and Safety Executive themselves. Again, **I Made It Happen!**

This is exactly how I operate, how I function. I make opportunities for myself. That is exactly what super-successful business people do.

You even have it written down in your notebook, **Make It Happen.** So, as you are now aware, when the American gold rush was created, many an opportunity was created too by some very smart individuals who never even got themselves dusty; they still made money, and vast amounts at that.

Later on you will read about RETENTION. I have placed that word in capitals for a very good reason. I would like you now to write that word on your noticeboard, also in large capital letters. You will understand the relevance of this very word later and the immense value it holds to you and your future success.

So just remember 'Picks & Shovels' situations and events create opportunities, they are all around you.

Chapter 14

Cash Is King and Always Will Be

In 1996 I was chosen to stunt double Ronnie Corbett on a feature film entitled *Fierce Creatures* staring John Cleese, Jamie Lee Curtis and Michael Palin. What I did not realise was that this very job would be key to an amazing financial future. The job, although not complicated, had its inherent difficulties as I was dressed in a seal suit and had to dive through a window. It was shot at Pinewood Studios and I was there for three weeks.

Fast forward now to 1998, when I was working on a television production in London called *An Unsuitable Job for a Woman*, playing the role of a skateboarding gang member. While having our afternoon break, my mobile telephone rang. I was asked if I was available to stunt double Ronnie Corbett on a Pizza Hut commercial. The dates in question fitted in perfectly with the production I was about to finish.

At the time I was still not a home-owner. I do have to stress the point that you do not own your home unless that you have purchased it outright with cash or paid off your mortgage; you DO NOT own your home if you have a mortgage as the bank owns it. I have stated this previously, I need to make that point very clear. I was living in Melton Mowbray with my (then) girlfriend but the relationship was not too great, so I needed to find my own place to live.

As you are aware I do not believe in borrowing money, never have, never will, we will discuss Debt Danger in a later chapter.

I was five years into my career. I was now an Intermediate Stuntman but had never worked on a television commercial before. However, I was well aware just how lucrative it could be. The Pizza Hut commercial was an amazing job for so many reasons, both professional and financial. The week's engagement would count towards my promotion to Stunt Co-ordinator and at this point I did not realise that my very first television commercial in 1998 would lead to 11 amazing years working in the most rewarding section of advertising that there is.

Equity, the actors' union, collaborated with the advertisers to create a contract which was referred to as the 1991 agreement, meaning that an actor or Stuntman who appeared on screen in front of camera was entitled to repeat fees. The payments in question were worked out by the artiste's daily rate. In 1998 my daily rate was £500 which was much higher than most Stunt Co-ordinators were charging.

Remember what I said in Chapter Eight? Know Your Worth. I had been charging £500 a day for every job I was engaged on as an Intermediate Stuntman whereas most of my colleagues were afraid to Know Their Worth. Why do Lamborghini and Ferrari charge a premium for their cars? They Know Their Worth. I am reliable, I do exactly what I say I can do, I am never late, EVER! I am honest, highly intelligent and highly skilled and those skills come at a price.

So if I had charged the standard £300 that other Stuntmen were being paid, my royalties would have been based on that figure and not on £500, a massive difference.

I have an excellent memory of difficult times from foraging for food in waste bins to walking those two miles each way and each day in all weathers in the 1980s to get a lift to work; from having very little money to survive, how hard I trained to become a Stuntman, seeing the Lamborghini Jalpa in a Nottingham car showroom, to witnessing individuals driving the streets in Ferraris. I had earned the right to be reassuringly expensive.

When the Pizza Hut commercial was first transmitted you could see Riky Ash being Ronnie Corbett diving out of a cat flap, roller skating up a garden path then vaulting over a collie dog in the street. It was going to run for six months, which was a considerable time for an ad campaign, however it actually ran for a year and a half, earning me a massive £75,000 in royalty payments alone. Today that would equate to around £185,000 (2024) and that does not include the week's wages plus stunt adjustments I received.

To give you an insight, a stunt adjustment is an additional payment on top of the daily fee for the added danger the job may entail. For example, if I charge my current £1200 daily rate and then I was required to perform a full fire burn, I would charge a stunt adjustment of £5000 per take, so if I was only required to do one take, I would receive a payment of £6200 for that day.

I banked every penny of my Pizza Hut commercial money, which I decided to use to purchase my first home. With my savings and investments, when the Pizza Hut money was banked and taxes paid, for the first time in my life I had over £100,000 in the bank; to the resentment of several of my colleagues, who had spent many a year wasting their earnings away thinking everyday would be payday. It just does not happen like that.

You MUST be prepared that not every year is going to be a Pizza Hut year. I was very astute to not spend my vast wealth on a property. What I actually did was look for more of an investment property that I could call home and then, when it had increased in value, I would sell at a massive profit. Remember 'Money Makes Money' Chapter 12.

Do enjoy your wealth; however, always be prepared and have what is referred to in the financial world as a buffer.

You MUST have at your disposal accessible savings – **Write It Down.**

So, in February 2000 I purchased my first-ever house outright with cash, yes cash, for £45,000. I did not use a solicitor or a conveyancer; I completed all the documentation myself by borrowing a book from the library entitled *House Buying Selling and Conveyancing* by Joseph Bradshaw ISBN 1-904053-29-7. What an absolutely amazing book, it gave me all the information necessary to buy and sell houses myself, priceless.

Knowledge is power; I advise you always to read and increase your financial knowledge.

Remember when the 'Negs' of society said I would never own a Lamborghini, establish my own business, become a Stuntman? Well, they were at it again, bailing copious amounts of shit out, like, you must use a solicitor to buy a house, and you cannot do it yourself. The Fucking Uneducated amongst us yet again, and yet again I proved them wrong; if you are purchasing your property using your own cash, not a mortgage, you can, and I did.

The seller accepted my offer of £45,000 although he was asking £50,000; good negotiation and having confidence saved me £5,000.

As soon as the seller realised I was a cash buyer it was worth his taking the £5000 hit to get the sale, and a sale that was completed in a record three weeks.

Now our once-great country has gone to shit for so many reasons and one reason that stands out is because of our corrupt government trying to force us to be a cashless society. The Shit4Brainz amongst us are yet again totally Fucking Clueless as to the damage they are doing to their financial future. When you pay for everything digitally your footprint is logged. Our corrupt government knows where and what you are spending your money on, that is why you should always pay by cash.

Let's look at a builder who takes a considerable volume of cash in payment for the work he does. It is totally his choice if he declares it; if he does not declare it what exactly do you think he does with the money?

He spends it, and if he decides not to declare it, he is saving himself tax, therefore he has more money to spend and that money then enters the system, making the economy stronger. Also, the person who has engaged him to do the work gets a much better deal from paying by cash, which again leaves them with more disposable income to spend which goes on to strengthen the economy.

When I was in Russia, if you dined in a restaurant there were two bills. The first bill you were presented with was if you wished to pay by card; the second bill was a much lower figure, to entice you to pay by cash. That is exactly what businesses want, payment by cash, that way they decide how much they feel they want to declare and by having a large quantity of cash at their disposal it affords them stronger negotiating power when making large purchases, again allowing money to enter back into the economy, making everyone considerably richer.

Back in the 1970s and 1980s, if you wanted a second-hand car, you approached a dealer and struck a favourable cash deal. The salesperson would then put a portion of the price of the car through the books and pocket the rest.

Again, that cash he received did not reside in his pocket, he spent it, thus pushing the cash back into the economy, making another person wealthy at the same time as making himself wealthy. You have better buying power when you have cash, as this happened with virtually anything you wanted to purchase as CASH was always KING.

Fortunately trading in this fashion still does happen today and businesses have realised that to endure in such harsh economic conditions they have to take a considerable volume of undeclared cash, purely to survive; businesses who fail to adopt this strategy, die, and die broke, and that is why so many businesses fail today.

If you have a cash economy, you have a very strong economy and that is exactly why Cash Is King and always will be – **Write It Down.**

Chapter 15

Prepare Yourself

I consider this to be by far the most important chapter in my book and for very good reason. Prepare Yourself!

Our oh so corrupt government does not want you to succeed, in fact, they desire you to fail and fail miserably, to be poorly paid, be racked in lifelong debt that will be impossible to clear and die broke, that is exactly what they want of you.

They do not want you to be financially free, to be independent, to be self-employed or a business owner; the only thing you are to them is cash, they need you to be subservient, to be their bitch and a miserable bitch at that. Are you one of the Sheeple of life who really believes what the government says?

Do you really believe that they are looking after your interests?

Every single thing you are told by the government has an agenda behind it. What you are told is not for your advantage, it is for the government's advantage so that they can destroy all hope of your ever becoming successful and financially free. Our corrupt government makes the laws and the rules for the benefit of themselves, NOT for YOU!

The government are The Shit On Your Shoes – **Write It Down.**

I was able to establish from a very young age that I was going to have many enemies in life and that the worst enemy I was going to face was our corrupt government. I established this thought process when I was as young as 19 and my opinion of them has been reinforced even more throughout my life to be correct. I have the confidence to stand up to their shite, Do You? To become super successful, you MUST be rebellious.

If our corrupt government tells me to walk through door A I am going through door B. Whatever they say I am doing the opposite because I know the shite they try to peddle to the people is for their benefit only and NOT MINE. I would never have the life I have today if I did not have the social intelligence to think this way. Everything I have done has paid off; did it pay off for my friends in the 1980s and my work colleagues who were racked in debt with ugly lives and ugly wives, because they lacked the courage to live their life their way?

The education system from comprehensive school and upwards is a complete failure. Our corrupt government pushes every child into university to keep the unemployment figures down, provided with easy access to finance that they will never be able to pay off. They then graduate with a degree not fit to wipe a tramp's ass with. Our failed education system is creating failures, weak-minded people with no confidence, with low self-esteem, no courage, no financial acumen and no Bollocks, just M.O.D.E.L. 'I have been offended', Fucking Useless children. This is because today children are teaching children, and by that, I mean teachers are far too young, with no life experience whatsoever and these so-called teachers are just children themselves. How Fucked Up is that?

Our corrupt government needs you to be a MODEL. Now in my amazing book *With Confidence* I educate the reader about what a MODEL citizen actually is, so for you this is exactly what you MUST avoid being:

Mediocre

Obedient

Dependent

Entertained

Lifeless

NEVER allow the government to control you – **Write It Down.**

To become independent and financially super successful you MUST NOT be a M.O.D.E.L. citizen, if you are any one of the above you WILL NOT ever become rich and you WILL NEVER become a Millionaire.

Here is a fine example and I could choose many others to amplify my point. I will use two examples of how stupid individuals fall into the M.O.D.E.L. trap.

First point, climate change. I ask you when did you first hear of this? Was it in the media by any chance? It was, who controls the media? Our corrupt government, who controls me? I do, I decide what I am going to believe NOT fall into the cesspit of being brainwashed, I am better than that and you need to be also.

You need to stop believing their shit, the title 'Climate Change' was created by the government who then feed their chosen agenda to the media who then feed it to you.

This is where choice comes in; the choice is yours, you can believe it, or you can reject it. What I will tell you is that this planet goes through what are referred to as Climate Cycles, just like our seasons, our planet is around four billion years old, we do not have any data from day one to the present day so when so-called scientists peddle climate change shite they are just talking out of their smelly asses, they are as pathetic as the very people who pull their strings, they are nothing but puppets.

Last week I was chatting with my web designer about my thoughts, and he agreed, adding that scientists are like those crazy people who have an imaginary friend by the name of God. He summed it up perfectly, scientists and religion are one and the same, they are all full of shit, believing in something that just does not exist.

When I saw Just Stop Oil glueing their ugly faces to the M25 do you know what I did? Firstly, I tried to find out what glue they were using as when I try to stick something I can never get the Fucker to hold.

Secondly, I bought shares in BP and Shell, and I am doing very well with them. Treat these ass holes as entertainment, just as I do when I witness an MP speaking, Nigel Farage excepted, as he is by far one of the very few members of parliament with any common sense, intelligence and courage to actually make this Shit Hole of a country better.

Remember to be super successful Attitude is Everything.

My next point, Electric Cars.

SHOW THE WORLD YOU KNOW FUCK ALL ABOUT MOTORING AND BUY ONE.

A fine example of the Shit4Brainz amongst us who have already made and regretted the most stupid purchase of their life. Why did they feel the need anyway to go electric? Apart from them being totally Fucking Clueless, they are exactly what our corrupt government need them to be M.O.D.E.L.

This is where the 'O' comes into play, **O**bedient. The Thick As Pig Shit amongst us hear the media feed them 'Fossil fuel is bad, you must now buy an electric car' and people actually believe this, well I DO NOT!

No Shit4Brainz MP or European Union are going to dictate to me what type of car I am going to drive and here is the interesting thing, I am never wrong, I predicted that electric vehicles would fail, and they have.

The gullible amongst us were enticed with free road tax, free on-street charging points, subsidised home chargers, now all gone, how dishonest is that.

Now say I buy a car for, let's say, £50,000. You buy an electric car at £50,000 and in five years' time I can assure you my car will be worth £60,000 and yours £6,000.

So, you want to become rich? Do not EVER buy an electric car!

If you are **D**ependent, you will NEVER be rich, you will forever be miserable and broke, remember WORK, CONSUME, DIE. That is exactly what our corrupt government requires of you, just another Brick In The Wall, **M**ediocre, being **E**ntertained with shit from Netflix, Amazon Prime, Disney and Apple TV, not only a waste of your valuable life, also a complete waste of money, Cancel Them NOW!

Concerts and festivals will also lose you money and make another person rich.

For the past 31 years, since 1993 I have worked extensively in the television and film industry. I know more about the industry than most, an industry that was great to work in, however it has been hijacked by the Snowflake WOKE brigade and that is exactly why you have shite viewing which just makes you **L**ifeless. Brainwashed and that is exactly what the government needs you to be, BRAINWASHED so they can control you.

Governments have no control whatsoever over confident, independent thinkers, the entrepreneurs of the world, those rare individuals like me who Make It Happen.

The very reason the government lowers the interest rate is to trap the Shit4Brainz to borrow money, instead of the individual working hard and investing and using hard earned cash to buy what they need; rather than doing this, our corrupt government wants you racked in debt, so much debt, in fact, that you will never pay it off. That is exactly why interest rates are so low, DO NOT EVER fall into the borrowing money trap, if you do you will be forever a slave. I am showing you how you can become a Millionaire by never ever borrowing money, I did it and so can you.

Whenever I invest, I NEVER consider the environment, what our corrupt government wants me to do; I do my research, establish what works for me and then commit.

It is exactly how I have become one of the most successful Stuntmen in the world today, I commit, if I say I am going to do something I do it, no matter what the odds, no matter what others say, no matter what laws I may break, I DO IT!

Never be a M.O.D.E.L. citizen; if you do, you will be forever poor. – **Write It Down.**

Mediocre

Obedient

Dependent

Entertained

Lifeless

The astute businessman pays low or no tax, yes you read that correctly. Let's take an average worker earning £25,000 per year. Their employer deducts, from their wages, income tax and national insurance and if they are as Thick As Pig Shit, a pension contribution too.

I will cover why you MUST never have a pension in a later chapter.

So, from their earnings of £25,000 they are left with around £21,000, which equates to around £400 per week.

Now what makes matters worse is our Shit4Brainz irresponsible government froze our personal allowance until 2028 which is currently locked at £12,570, meaning that you will pay more tax.

Now let's look at a self-employed person who earns £25,000 per year. They can very easily pay no tax whatsoever when they take into account their expenses allowance for being a self-employed person. When an employed person drives to work, they cannot claim their motoring expenses whereas a self-employed person can and is also able to claim for tools and materials, whereas an employed person does not have this right. A self-employed person pays Class 2 National Insurance which is considerably less than the Class 1 which an employed person needs to pay.

An employed person has a set wage and possibly overtime, a self-employed person sets their own rates and the hours they choose to work.

Now you can see why the government wants you to be a M.O.D.E.L. citizen.

How would you feel if you were constantly lied to, given false promises and ultimately led to fail? How would you feel? If you have children, would you bring them up to lie, cheat, steal? I hope not, so why do you tolerate such behaviour on a daily basis from our government?

You know when you see journalists ask questions of members of the public in the street, because I work in the media, I know they vet the answers to match up with the programme's point of view. On one occasion a woman was asked her thoughts on leaving the European Union; now before I continue any further, I have a very important point to make.

When David Cameron was urging the people of this country to vote to remain in the corrupt European Union, through desperation he dragged Barack Obama over from the US of A, and had the governor of the Bank of England, Mark Carney, both begging us to vote remain and what did we do? We said to ourselves, 'You do not tell us what to do, we will do what we feel is best for us and our country' so we voted to leave.

What we did, was give David Cameron a right good kick in the teeth, so hard that he never recovered and still to this day remains in a political coma, consistently pissing his pants when he hears the words, 'We Won.'

As you are very well aware, the government wants me to walk through door A. I am walking through door B, as I am very well aware that absolutely everything the government does is to weaken and undermine us.

Now back to the woman in the street, when asked how she would vote her answer was as follows, 'If the government says we must vote remain they must know better than me so I will vote as they tell me to.'

Shit4Brainz in action, there is a fine example of 'Work Consume Die,' mentally a useless fucker going nowhere fast.

From now on you are always going to go through Door B.

If I had been weak enough to listen to our corrupt government, I certainly would not have the life I have today.

The government wants you to lack confidence, have low expectations and low self-worth, that way they have full control over you.

Remember what I said, you need to be the Shepherd and NOT the sheep.

Always remind yourself that they will forever be, **The Shit On Your Shoes!**

Chapter 16

The Danger Of Debt

Never believe there is such a thing as good debt, there is not. When you borrow money, you instantly become a slave and have burdened yourself. Now you have choices, either pay some or all of the borrowed money back, plus interest, or pay nothing.

I must enlighten you, borrowing money with no intention of repaying it is theft. Never be that person, the utter scum who traverse through life, lying, cheating and stealing.

I would ban borrowing money in every form possible if I was in power. It is unnecessary and a greedy way to live. As you are aware I have become a Millionaire without ever borrowing money. I have proved it can be done. I am sure those of you who have a mortgage or are considering obtaining one will disagree with me, saying that this is the only way to get onto the property ladder. Well, you are wrong. You can, if you are willing to make sacrifices and start modestly. There are relatively affordable properties out there that you can purchase outright with cash, yes cash that you have saved.

In 2000 I purchased a two-bedroom semi-detached house in Nottingham, valued at £50,000, for £45,000. The moment I moved in I was already £5,000 in profit. I was willing to get my hands dirty and renovate it all by myself.

Six years later I sold that very house for £107,000, making a profit of £62,000. During the six years of my occupancy, I undertook the renovations myself as well as working extensively as a Stuntman and Stunt

The Danger Of Debt

Co-ordinator. By doing this myself, I was able to save considerably more money.

Now I know interest rates are currently 1% of Fuck All! and this is for good reason. The Shit4Brainz amongst us borrow, rack up debt that they will never be able to repay, **Work Consume** and then **Die Broke**, again all fuelled by our corrupt government.

They want you in debt, to be their bitch, that is exactly why they structure the interest rates to be so low. Even if the interest rates were 10% that is still far too low. What people seem to easily forget is that inflation erodes your money. Also, there is never a guarantee that the property for which you have obtained the mortgage will increase in value.

Are you aware of Negative Equity? Your investment is worth far less than you paid for it.

In 1997 I dated a girl who I eventually moved in with; at the time, as a research and development scientist for a famous crisp manufacturer, she earned £500 per week, equivalent to £1100 today (2024), a very well-paid lady. Now one would think that being a scientist she would have some acumen when it came to money.

Now this lady in question earned in a year £26,000, equivalent to £58,000 today (2024), yet she was broke, and I mean broke, why? Because she had no ability to retain her wealth.

Retention Is Better Than Poor – **Write It Down.**

It is not the amount of money that you earn that matters, it is the amount of money you retain from the money you earn that really matters.

So, my girlfriend was earning £26,000 per year and was broke, she may as well have earned nothing as everything she had she did not even own; negative equity with her maisonette which she mortgaged well over what it was worth, her new motorbike financed, holidays paid for on a credit card, all requiring to be paid off, she became a slave and she created that slave life for herself.

In Life You Make Your Own Heaven and You Make Your Own Hell – **Write It Down.**

On her high salary, she could easily have saved and bought her first house outright with cash, like I did, and, ironically, she watched me do exactly that.

So, who is better off, a person earning £50,000 per year who, after their lavish lifestyle, is left with nothing but debt, or a person earning £15,000 per year who manages to save £5,000?

It is not the amount of money that you earn that matters, it is the amount of money you retain from the money you earn that really matters.

Our corrupt government sets you up to fail, there are even several payment plans put forward when you are looking to make domestic purchases and the Shit4Brainz who take out these payday loans and payment plans then have the audacity to blame the companies providing them when they cannot meet the payments. That is how Fucked Up this pathetic country has become; you MUST take responsibility for your actions.

You do not have to borrow money, you do not need a credit card, what you need to do is work hard and that is what the current generation are not prepared to do.

Life is hard, do not make it any more difficult for yourself by obtaining loans.

I also do have to blame Martin Lewis for some of this; on his ITV money show he is always pushing 'Credit Score.' I have no idea what my credit score is, and I simply do not care and nor should you.

Credit reference agencies should be abolished. Established by our corrupt government to spy on us, try opening a bank account today; it is virtually impossible because of the damage credit reference agencies do.
Remember Confidence is the motivator for life. Having the confidence to live your life your way, NOT the way our corrupt government wants you to live.

Debt will destroy you and there is already enough out there in life doing a good job trying to destroy you too, you do not need another enemy, one is more than enough. The only way of achieving financial freedom is by NEVER borrowing money.

If you really want something work hard for it, look at your vision board every day, think when you are travelling on 'The Looser Cruiser' to work of a Monday morning how much better you can make your life and not the life our corrupt government wants you to live in a miserable existence. Most people are not prepared to work hard to make their life better, just settling for a M.O.D.E.L. life and miserable existence.

Be patient, establish savings and investments alongside creating multiple income streams, put in the effort the application deserves, and you will have more money than you will know what to do with, now is that not better than harbouring life-long debt?

It Can Be Done and I Will Do It – **Write It Down.**

Chapter 17

Multiple Income Streams

By 2006 I had created several income streams, however I knew I needed to establish more. One of my major earners was my extensive work on television commercials, from my Pizza Hut commercial in 1998, stunt doubling Ronnie Corbett, to working on some of the most prestigious ad campaigns ever.

One memorable experience was becoming 'The Tango Man' on a Tango commercial, being hauled up to a magnet 50 feet above the ground wearing a diver's helmet filled with oranges and then being dropped back to earth and the oranges were now orange juice and the caption, "You Know When You've Been Tango'ed" appears. One of the most memorable television commercials ever.

Now to secure this very commercial I had to attend two auditions in London. The first was against five of my colleagues. We all differed in look, however we all had the ability to do what was required of us, the application.

Being an expert in body language and psychoanalysis, I provide myself with the added advantage of not only displaying a positive and confident persona, but also being able to read the room. I project success, you have the right person for the job and this ability has paid off for me many times. My relaxed, let's say, 'Could not care less' manner nails it for me every time and I had this one securely pinned down.

Once again I negotiated a very high daily rate and insisted I was placed upon the 1991 Television Commercials Agreement which secured me royalties for life. I am a smart businessman and always look towards my future.

From casting, meetings, rehearsal to the actual shoot day leading to one of the most memorable ad campaigns ever, being 'The Tango Man' was amazing. These are the jobs I enjoy most, the solo jobs, just me, cast and crew. From a very young age I worked much better alone, and Kung-Fu teaches one to be solitary. I am answerable to no one.

By concentrating on television work and mainly television commercials I created for myself <u>Multiple Income Streams</u> and you must create these for yourself too.

Times have changed. The 'Job For Life' no longer exists, no one can accurately predict our future. At school one was encouraged into what was referred to as a 'Job For Life'.

A person would leave school and work in a bank as a clerk and eventually through good work be promoted to manager. Even if one did not have those ambitions, one was safe in the understanding that there would always be a job at the bank until one retired at 60 or 65.

Life is not like that anymore; the uncertainty of employment and even self-employment means that to reach the target of Millionaire, you can no longer rely on a 'Job For Life'.

I MUST create for myself Multiple Income Streams – **Write It Down.**

Even as far back as my cabinet-making days I had exploited the value of <u>Multiple Income Streams</u>. In addition to the wages I received as a cabinet maker, I did what was referred to as jobs on the side, whether that was making things for people or doing flat felt roofing and decorating or driving Helen the stripper around; they were all income streams that I had created and I was willing to do the most important thing and Work Hard.

If you are a practical person, you should be able to turn your hand to absolutely anything and that is the way to create Multiple Income Streams.

Look at all of your qualities, all of your earning potential, what can you do to bring in extra cash? If you already have an occupation, unless you are in the £100,000 plus earning bracket, you will need Multiple Income Streams to become a Millionaire.

Alongside my work as a Stuntman, I am also a Stunt Co-ordinator, I am an actor, an author, an international speaker, a Kung-Fu instructor, an expert witness. I am also in the process of creating a YouTube channel as The Strategist, to help young guys become super successful and smash this pathetic WOKE Snowflake society we are being forced to reside in.

You DO NOT have to conform.

Entrepreneurs will always have Multiple Income Streams; they will invest in several businesses and when they feel that a business is close to reaching its 'sell by date' they have already established their next venture.

From first becoming a Stuntman in 1993 I was regularly asked the same question: 'How do you become a Stuntman?' I would always take the time to answer the question, this took a considerable amount of my time as I would receive telephone calls from individuals who aspired to break into the film and television industry. This led to an idea; how do I provide people with the information they require to become Stuntmen and alleviate the burden on my precious time?

I was reading *Max Power* car magazine and noticed, amongst all the Quick 'Jerk Off' adds by Sophie Tit Wank, that there were some information lines. I cultivated an idea, what if I recorded a message with all the information required for one to know what they needed to do to train to become a Stuntman and this could then be promoted through a premium rate 09 telephone number? This would help the person who was seriously interested in becoming a Stuntman and at the same time free up my time to run my businesses and live my life.

It worked. I narrated all the required information and advertised the 09 number in various magazines and the money flowed in. It cost £1.50 per minute to call the number and out of that I received £1.11; another income stream that made me money while I slept.

The beauty of my Stunt Information Line was that if any of the criteria changed, I just recorded a more up to date message. I also promoted my Stunt Information Line on the 'Contact' page of my website.

That is what being an entrepreneur is all about, you have to seek out those opportunities that are all around you, exploit them and **MAKE IT HAPPEN!**

As I have stated and will continue to state throughout all of my work, you MUST be prepared to Work Hard!

I had created Multiple Income Streams even before the internet was established, and you now have so much more opportunity to create for yourself your very own Multiple Income Streams.

What I have done is to make myself Future Proof; by that I mean I have established for myself income streams that are diverse in the way that each are separate, so if the film and television industry goes quiet and work slows down, I have other things I can do.

Also, my investments all produce additional income. It is having several income streams and wise investments that enabled me in 2006 to sell my two-bedroom semi-detached house in Nottingham and move to a four-bedroom executive home in Lincolnshire that I bought outright with cash for £250,000, again no mortgage. As I stated, it can be done and I did it, which again always reminds me of those individuals who wrote me off. Who's laughing now? Fuck Em as my good friend Roger always says.

I sold my home in Nottingham without the aid of an estate agent. I made my very own For Sale board and, as my house was located within walking distance of the City Hospital, I made some sales brochures and pinned them to every noticeboard in the hospital. After less than a week of doing this, I had secured a buyer, a nurse who was looking for a starter home. Again, through astuteness I Made It Happen.

Throughout the whole selling and buying process I did not use a solicitor, again turning to Joseph Bradshaw's amazing book *House Buying Selling and Conveyancing* to guide me through the process. Having the confidence to carry all of this out myself I attribute to my amazing confidence. I have a saying, 'If A Man Can Do It, A Man Can Do It', meaning that if a man learned that very skill so can I.

I have saved myself over £15,000 in the buying and selling process by not employing solicitors, estate agents and conveyancers and taking those job roles on myself, which resulted in my getting the job done much quicker, and another talent added to my list.

So, through hard work, dedication and self-belief I was now the owner of a £250,000 home which equates to £487,000 today (2024), the house purchased outright with cash created through one of my many income streams.

It can be done.

Today you cannot rely on one income stream as we live in such a volatile environment.

So, on your journey to Millionaire status, start establishing those <u>Multiple Income Streams</u> as they are the foundation of your financial future.

Chapter 18

Surround Yourself With Success

Now when I was in my teenage years and established that I wanted to be rich and super successful, I did not know any successful people. However, regardless of that I still endured and achieved every goal I set myself, that is down to having a determined personality that no matter what, I will always win.

Now if, at this stage in your life, you do not yet possess the personality required to be super successful, I suggest that you start now to surround yourself with success, be around successful people at every opportunity. People who are self-made will never object to you being around them if you are honest about your intentions.

The closest I ever got when in my teenage years was visiting supercar showrooms and driving past Millionaire mansions. Even though I was self-motivated I still surrounded myself with success, I would read magazines aimed at the wealthy at a time when my friends were wasting their life away in the bars and clubs around Nottingham.

Try where possible to surround yourself with positive, successful individuals, ones who have a story to tell. I very much enjoy hearing about people's success and how they achieved great wealth. I know what it is like to be broke, to be poor, to have nothing, to be cold and hungry. I knew there was more for me in life, I read books, listened to cassettes of very successful people's journeys. Yes, when most lads my age were listening to music while they drove, I was listening to motivational speakers, successful businessmen who inspired me.

I stood outside in the pouring rain looking into supercar showrooms, knowing that one day I would succeed. I never had the right kind of people around me; I did not know anyone who was super successful, and I still made it, no internet to inspire me, just that strong desire to better myself. You must never let anyone grind you down to their level. If they lack confidence, intelligence and humour and the motivation to better themselves and be super successful, then that is their problem. If you have to mix and communicate with the Shit4Brainz in life, make it as brief as you possibly can.

I was criticised for focusing my energy towards becoming successful and even ostracised, which is what I expect of low life, going nowhere fast mentalities, those very people who end up working for people with ambition.

Seek out Those You Admire, Those Who Inspire – **Write It Down.**

Also never forget the power of visualisation, those individuals who inspire you to become the best person you can possibly be, imagine just how different your life is going to be when you achieve your desired goals.

Your vision board should be your first and last focus every waking day. If it is not possible for you to seek out successful people, watch the many motivational videos and success stories on the internet on various platforms. You will observe that no matter what their backstory, no matter what type of business they pursued, you will see that all super successful Millionaires and Multi-Millionaires have the very same traits, which we will come to in a later chapter; for you to succeed on your journey to Millionaire status you MUST have all the characteristics and qualities that make successful people achieve.

As much as I love my job as a Stuntman, unfortunately the film and television industry is a cesspit of negativity. No matter what job I work on, the cast and crew I am surrounded by are mostly negative, they are not my kind of people.

Surround Yourself With Success

I have to work alongside them and, listening to their conversations about their life and life in general, they all seem to be clueless, inadequate and broke, and have no financial skills whatsoever. It is this left-wing Thick As Pig Shit attitude that has resulted in their failure and lack of success which has led them on to a miserable existence.

I am never affected by their pessimism; I am just glad I am me!

You cannot have a positive life with a negative mind.

My analogy is that most people are insecure and wish they had the confidence to be free to speak their mind. Sadly, the television and film industry has been destroyed by W.O.K.E.ism and as you very well know, Go W.O.K.E. and you will certainly Go BROKE!

And that is exactly what has happened to our television and film industry, it is broken beyond repair.

If I had listened to the negative influence of others, I would not have the amazing life I have today. Even to this very day I still surround myself with success and you must do that too.

Chapter 19

RIKY X

In 2009 I was sitting at Heathrow airport, waiting to catch a flight to Sicily to be part of one of the most amazing experiences of my career. I was going to be playing the role of an Italian racing driver on a Ferrari commercial. It is moments like these that remind me of how hard life was and if I had not motivated myself, worked hard and I mean hard, I would not be living the life I am.

When you apply yourself and are prepared to endure the knockbacks, the negativity and make sacrifices, in time the hard work pays off.

There was I, waiting for my first-class flight, going to be part of a Ferrari commercial. In January 2009 I was asked to attend an audition in London, not realising at the time that the production company was seeing in excess of 70 Stuntmen. Regardless of this I have a unique way of approaching the inconvenience of auditioning; I tell myself that they are seeing only me and that no matter what, I am without question the best Stuntman for the job and often I am.

I enter the room with confidence. Now if you are Ferrari, you hope that the Stuntman that you engage can handle not only an audition, also the intense action you have scripted.

Out of the 70 Stuntmen seen over three days the job was mine. I had nailed it, to the anger, resentment and jealousy of some of my colleagues, which is exactly what I expect of certain negative people. I would never expect them to have a good word to say about me.

As you progress towards Millionaire status, if you are not mentally and physically strong you will be destroyed. You have to be tough because sadly in life most people want to see you fail rather than praise you for your efforts, 'Fuck Em.'

Working for three weeks in Sicily was simply amazing. I had worked hard throughout my career and in time it pays off, another commercial to list on my CV.

Ironically fast forward to July 2009 and again I am sitting in the departure lounge at Heathrow heading off to Romania to work on a Heineken commercial.

Just before I left home to travel to Heathrow Airport to fly out to Romania, a package arrived, which I placed in my travel bag to open while I awaited my flight. I had no idea what the package contained. On opening it I pulled out a book entitled *Secret of My Success* by business journalist Jamie X Oliver – no, not the chef. Jamie had spent several years travelling the world, interviewing thousands of businessmen and women. He then wrote a book featuring the most successful. Jamie had telephoned me in 2007, while working for *The Daily Telegraph*, to write a feature about my life and success as a Stuntman and Stunt Co-ordinator. *The Daily Telegraph* ran the story in 2007.

As I looked through the book I came across Bill Gates, Richard Branson, Rocco Forte; and among these Business Greats I noticed my own name, Riky Ash, in the Networking Section of Jamie's book. There I was, Stuntman Riky, with my company "Falling For You" profiled alongside Richard Branson and Bill Gates.

Could life get any better?

In life I find it is very rare that one receives the credit and appreciation for one's work that one deserves, especially when one is a Stuntman. We are expected to make actors and actresses look great then dissolve away to be forgotten. Not Riky Ash, NO WAY!

I was so proud and humbled to have been selected as one of the world's most successful business people, bearing in mind that Bill Gates and Richard Branson would have received a copy of the book and would have been equally as excited to have been featured alongside Riky Ash. Jamie's book was simply amazing, very rewarding to anyone who aspires to be successful in business; each entrepreneur's story provided an insight into the highs and lows we all suffer in our business life.

In 2000 I had been honoured in The Guinness Book of Records; now in 2009 I again received world fame in Jamie's book. As I sat at Heathrow reading through the many stories, I reflected on every ten years to see exactly where my life had taken me. Back in 1999 I had just become a Stunt Co-ordinator after many years working as a successful Stuntman. I was preparing to purchase my first home outright with cash. Ten years earlier in 1989 I was representing Britain as a successful Kung-Fu fighter as well as being a very successful cabinet maker.

In 1989 I was having so much fun. Being in my early 20s I was not wealthy, although I possessed great self-belief that one day not only would I be successful, I would have a major impact in television and film. Here I was at Heathrow airport, departing soon to Romania, 16 years into my stunt career, a cabinet maker by trade, a Shaolin Kung-Fu expert and instructor, a Stuntman, Stunt Co-ordinator and actor, a speaker and published author.

My passion for exotic cars also extends to vehicle registration plates. Today we see so many interesting plates promoting a company or organisation or just an individual with their initials.

Now whatever business you choose to be your platform to success you MUST promote yourself in a professional manner. Now this may sound straightforward and obvious however there are so many businesses out there that are totally fucking clueless when it comes to marketing.

Firstly, they do not even have a professional email address, choosing gmail, hotmail, aol and yahoo. You MUST purchase for yourself a professional email address that not only represents your company, but must also promote it.

When I established 'Falling For You' I sought a designer for my letterheads, business cards and brochures; even the sleeves of my DVDs for my showreel were professionally designed. Alongside those, a professional website designed and managed by a full-time webmaster, NOT a friend who claims they can make a four-page site and does not have a Scooby Doo what The Fuck they are doing.

Your business MUST be seen to be professional at all times – **Write It Down.**

If you were shopping on the high street, how tempted would you be to enter a shoddy-looking dirty shop without signage as opposed to one with a more inviting aspect?

Just before I left for Bucharest, Romania, to work on the Heineken commercial, I was looking at investment registration plates. Remember when I touched on investments; from 1995 I decided to invest in personalised registration plates which have afforded me amazing returns. If I saw an old car rusting away on a driveway, I would ask the owner if they would sell me the registration plate. Before I made my offer, I would have it valued and establish its true worth, and if the owner was astute, they could have carried out these investigations themselves; however most who I approached did not.

I struck deals, purchasing registration plates for £200 that today are worth in excess of £5,000. I am able to advertise them fee-free and take a healthy return.

The then girlfriend had found R1KY X, showed it to me and got my mind thinking, what an amazing asset to 'Falling For You' as I spell Riky without a 'c'.

I made a low offer before I left for Bucharest, enjoyed my backwards stair fall in the military circle, which is very historic in Romanian history, and my Stunt Co-ordinating various fights. On returning home my low offer, to my surprise, had been accepted.

Now registration plates may not be your passion. I had done for my business two things; I had purchased another appreciating asset which was also a great advertisement for my business. Image is everything, remember what I said about the shoddy high street store.

The way you present yourself represents your success – **Write It Down.**

Never be shy to shine, I am very proud of what I have achieved and happily show off. I have arrived many times in my Lamborghini for stunt jobs and received mixed reactions. I do not care what anyone thinks, I worked hard for my success and have every right to be flash. I endure, no matter what, and you need to too.

Many times, when I park up in my Lamborghini, meet with so-called friends I have not seen for some time or just in passing meet an acquaintance I used to know from years gone by, they see the car I drive and their response is, 'It's all right for some.'

This just makes me realise just how lazy and unmotivated people are when they say this. Do they really think that my Lamborghini dropped out of the sky with my home and all the other possessions I have worked so hard for, and I emphasise the word WORK? I have not won, inherited, found, stolen or been given anything in this life; I have earned every penny I have through my own dedication, courage and hard work, and my Very Smart approach to finance. As you know, I have developed The Midas Touch.

Remember the shoe salesmen's reactions, one positive the other negative? Your reaction when you witness success is to be positive and motivated, ask how did you afford that car? What is it that you do? I still ask Lamborghini owners who I meet when I have my car serviced and at events, they inspire me, I want to know what journey they travelled to afford such luxuries. However, if they do not own their car, by that I mean the finance company owns it, I am not impressed as anyone can rack themselves in debt, cutting out the hard work, Work Hard mentality.

RIKY X

Now look at your vision board, also your notebook, you are setting yourself up for success, enjoy every second of it, because you are a long time dead.

You were born to shine.

RIKY X is now proudly displayed on my Lamborghini Gallardo Spyder.

Chapter 20

Attitude Is Everything

Throughout my life, right up to this very day I have met more negative people than positive. I am astute enough to know those who are my kind of people; now successful people all think in the same way, we all have very similar personality traits and we are resilient.

I am going to list for you what makes a person wealthy and successful. Attitude Is Everything – **Write It Down.**

Now throughout my Kung-Fu training I have been taught that I am the absolute best and no matter what, I cannot be defeated and will always endure. It was ironic that even before my Kung-Fu days, I had a positive Make It Happen personality; remember my reaction when I first saw the Lamborghini Jalpa.

I have so much self-belief, I have never in my life met anyone who has as much confidence as I do, I firmly believed I am without doubt the most confident man in the world today.

For you to be successful you MUST believe in yourself.

So, let's look at what makes a person successful:

Successful people have an aim.

Successful people mix with positive people.

Successful people know what they want.

Successful people are not shy.

Attitude Is Everything

Successful people create their own set of rules.

Successful people manage their money well.

Successful people are good at receiving compliments.

Successful people tend to be very brave.

Successful people are consistently learning and progressing.

Successful people admire other rich and successful people.

Successful people always create opportunities.

Successful people focus on the solution not the problem.

Successful people believe in their ability.

Successful people have a positive mental attitude.

Successful people are different.

Successful people have self-discipline.

Successful people win or learn and accept that.

Successful people are resilient.

Successful people take responsibility for their actions.

Successful people are committed.

Successful people are excellent at generating income.

Successful people have good people around them.

Successful people know their value.

What I now would like you to do is write out the list in your book.

Remember – **Write It Down.**

When you have written all 25 traits down, I need you to be completely honest with yourself and put a tick next to the characteristics you already possess.

Then put a red line under the traits you need to develop. We can now work through each one in more detail to help you progress.

SUCCESSFUL PEOPLE HAVE AN AIM

If you are going on a journey you need to know exactly how to get there; you also need to establish where exactly your destination will be and the same can be said of your journey to Millionaire status and super success. You MUST have an aim. 'I would like' is not the dialogue you should be using, you need to say, 'I am going to achieve.'

When I look back on my life, I have achieved everything I aimed for, from leaving school and becoming a cabinet maker, I had an aim to get a job, when I secured that job, I had an aim to become skilful as a craftsman.

In 1988 I had an aim to not only start Kung-Fu, even when attending my very first class my aim was to become a First Dan Red Sash. When I achieved this, I set my aim even higher and today am an Eighth Dan Shaolin Kung-Fu Grandmaster and my aim now is to become Tenth Dan Doctor of Shaolin Kung-Fu, and I will achieve this.

The same with becoming a Stuntman, I achieved through extreme hard work that goal in 1993; however, when I became a Stuntman, my aim was to become a Stunt Co-ordinator.

I always have an aim.

SUCCESSFUL PEOPLE MIX WITH POSITIVE PEOPLE

The people you choose to have around you have a massive influence on every aspect of your life. No matter how positive you are, being around a negative person will in time create a miserable existence for you.

You MUST always have successful people in your life and keep your association with negative people to an absolute minimum. If that means having very few friends, then that is exactly how it will be.

I have fewer than five real friends, who are all positive and successful. Positive people will help and support you and provide you with the correct advice and will be happy to see you succeed, trade ideas and will not suffer from that appalling disease by the name of jealousy.

Surround yourself with success and in time you too will be super successful.

SUCCESSFUL PEOPLE KNOW WHAT THEY WANT

Throughout my life I have always known what I wanted; I make solid decisions, I never procrastinate. You MUST know exactly what you want, otherwise you will be going nowhere fast!

Remember why super successful people have vision boards: it is because they know what they want, they know how to achieve and that is exactly what they do, no excuses, we achieve. I never use the phrase 'I'm not sure.' I am always sure. I know exactly what to do and when to do it. Set daily, weekly, monthly and yearly goals and if the vision board is filling up, create a second one.

SUCCESSFUL PEOPLE ARE NOT SHY

If you are shy, success is not for you, because to become super successful you have to believe in yourself, believe you are the absolute best and stand out. Successful people Make It Happen and if you suffer from shyness, you will never be able to Make It Happen. You have to ask questions. Shy people struggle with the basics of communication; you have to be prepared to complain and put slackers in their place. You have to have the confidence to present yourself, because if you come across as shy, no one will be interested in investing their time and knowledge in you as they will simply see it as a complete waste of time.

SUCCESSFUL PEOPLE CREATE THEIR OWN SET OF RULES

This is the foundation of becoming super successful and a Millionaire. You have to create for yourself your very own set of rules. If that means breaking our pathetic laws, then so be it. Let me explain it to you in the clearest terms possible, no one ever made a million pounds honestly as it is simply not possible.

You have to create your own set of rules for life. I started to create mine as far back as 1987 when I was able to establish just how corrupt our government was. If I had not possessed the courage to be rebellious, I would not have become a Millionaire. I cannot be controlled so rules and laws do not apply to me. My own set of rules work on the principle of super success. I am not influenced in any way by alleged climate change and utter bollocks that our shitty government doles out.

As I stated they DO NOT want you to be successful, they demand that you are their 'Bitch' and an obedient bitch at that.

You have to establish what works for you, adopt that way of thinking into every aspect of your life and you WILL become a Millionaire, fail to create your very own set of rules for your life, no matter how outrageous they are, or you will DIE BROKE.

SUCCESSFUL PEOPLE MANAGE THEIR MONEY WELL

Why is a person who earns £75,000 per year and lives as if they earn £80,000 always broke?
Or a person who earns £20,000 per year and manages to save and invest £10,000 rich?

I am no Carol Vodaphone, however I can deduce that no matter how much money you earn, if you do not possess that vital asset of being able to retain it, you will never become rich.

Retention Is Better Than Poor – **Write It Down.**

The more money that you can retain the richer you will become. When I was a cabinet maker earning £75 per week in 1987 I was driving around in a BMW, paid for outright with cash, while my work colleagues and friends were having to take 'The Loser Cruiser' to work, so why was this? Simply because I had the ability to appreciate the value of my money and make my money work hard for me. My friends and my colleagues, however, did not, getting pissed out of their ugly faces nearly every night of the week and wondering why they had such a shit life. For every pound I earned, I retained as much as I possibly could, I managed my money well, even when I was poorly paid, every penny counted and even today every penny still counts.

Learn the fine art of managing your money, investing it and making your money make money, that way you become rich even while you sleep.

SUCCESSFUL PEOPLE ARE GOOD AT RECEIVING COMPLIMENTS

I have never understood why certain individuals have trouble with accepting compliments. If you do well I will tell you, if you do badly, I will also tell you.

I do not need anyone to tell me I am good, I know I am; however, I do receive compliments very well. I deserve them for everything I have achieved in my life. Compliments, however rare they can be, are a motivator, a driver to even greater success. Remember that far too many people would rather put you down than praise you for your efforts, so be grateful for every compliment that comes your way.

SUCCESSFUL PEOPLE TEND TO BE VERY BRAVE

Bravery is an asset to being successful as you will be faced with many challenges. You will have to stand up to people and be direct. I have to do this so much in my working day, you have to be both mentally and physically strong, remember 'Create for yourself your very own set of rules'; it takes a brave person to stand up to our corrupt government, to have the courage to break our pathetic, not fit for purpose laws. Brave people are successful people, bravery brings great rewards, Be Brave.

SUCCESSFUL PEOPLE ARE CONSISTENTLY LEARNING AND PROGRESSING

Have you ever heard the saying, 'Every day's a school day'? You learn every day of your life. I immerse myself in knowledge every day, I am an avid reader, which broadens my intellect. I ask questions to learn, I watch videos, and I learn, which then makes me even more marketable. I use every resource possible to better myself and to progress. When you pass your driving test, for many years after you are still learning. Remember these wise words:

Knowledge Is Power – **Write It Down.**

SUCCESSFUL PEOPLE ADMIRE OTHER RICH AND SUCCESSFUL PEOPLE

I am inspired when I see a Ferrari or Lamborghini, or I drive past a million-pound mansion. Success motivates me and I deeply admire anyone who has worked hard and made it, they are my kind of people. As you know, when I had nothing, and I mean nothing, in life I drove my £300 van past million-pound mansions, I embraced success, made visits to supercar dealerships when I could not even afford the car's logo let alone the car itself, I still exposed myself to the trappings of success. My friends stared into the windows of Ford dealerships, while I was looking at Ferraris. Yes, my friends did laugh, however who's laughing now? Fuck Em!

SUCCESSFUL PEOPLE ALWAYS CREATE OPPORTUNITIES

Opportunities are all around you. I spoke to a multi-Millionaire back in the 1980s who made his fortune by going to carpet manufacturers and taking all the offcuts of the various flooring away for free. The companies thought he was doing them a favour as they did not then have to pay for their disposal. This smart guy at the time was also driving around in an old van. He then took the remnants and sold them on the market. What he had done was create an opportunity for himself to make money, enough money to become a Millionaire.

When I became a Stuntman, I was surprised that no one was trading in equipment. I saw an opportunity so I approached a fire clothing company and had them create fire clothing for stunt work, which I then went on to sell to stunt professionals. I also did the same with climbing and abseiling equipment and body armour. Each stunt engagement became an opportunity. I would showcase my wares and take sales on the day. I later created fire training days where stunt professionals could come to my Fire House and learn, which afforded me the opportunity once again to showcase my stock, which resulted in sales.

Create opportunities and you create wealth – **Write It Down.**

SUCCESSFUL PEOPLE FOCUS ON THE SOLUTION NOT THE PROBLEM

You are driving along, and you get a puncture, where do you direct your energy? The problem or the solution? Where should you direct your energy? The problem or the solution? Your energy should always be directed towards the solution NOT the problem. You cannot change what has happened, the only thing you can change is your reaction. Positive people focus on the solution, yes in life Shit happens! It always will, that is the nature of the beast, focus your energy on the solution and NOT the problem and you will always be on **The Winning Side.**

SUCCESSFUL PEOPLE BELIEVE IN THEIR ABILITY

If you do not believe in yourself, how can you expect others to believe in you? No place for modesty if you yearn to be super successful and a Millionaire. I knew when I was training to become a Stuntman that I would make an excellent Stuntman and would shine. When I qualified and was asked if I could do a car knockdown I aways answered yes, even when I had never done one, because I believed in myself and my ability, I knew I had what it takes. Same with my speaking work, I have the ability to be clear and concise and deliver powerful messages which resonate with my audience because I have exceptional ability.

Believe in your ability and nothing will stop you achieving your goals.

SUCCESSFUL PEOPLE HAVE A POSITIVE MENTAL ATTITUDE

This is an interesting one, some people struggle with positivity and others don't. From a very young age I have always been positive, I knew I would be successful. I handled knockbacks very well and never took cruel words personally. I developed the 'Nothing Ruffles My Feathers' attitude, remember sticks and stones may break my bones but names will never hurt me. Positivity makes you successful in every aspect of your life.

How positive do you think you need to be to jump off an 80-foot cliff? I can only win or learn, I can never fail and that is exactly how positive people think. I will always find a way no matter what and no matter what people think of me. I am self-motivated and you need to be too. You MUST always be positive even in the most testing of situations that life will throw your way.

Even on the coldest and darkest of winter days I am still positive because at some point the sun is gonna shine. Nothing positive ever comes from a negative mind.

Look at your vision boards, read your notes in your book; they all represent positivity.

It is the positive mental attitude that is going to be your fuel on your long journey to success and becoming a Millionaire.

SUCCESSFUL PEOPLE ARE DIFFERENT

I am proud to be different, look at the most influential people in history, they have all been unique: Oliver Cromwell, Isaac Newton, Harland Saunders, Donald Trump, Nigel Farage and Andrew Tate. Super successful. They were never concerned with what others thought of them and never cared what they said, and if the low life Shit4Brainz feel offended, Fuck Em!

You cannot offend anyone, it is simply not possible, and I will give you an example. If a woman is called a useless fat slag and she takes offence at those words, then she is reinforcing that she is fat that she is useless and that she is a slag.

If she brushes off those words and it does not resonate with her then she is bullet proof as she does not believe the dialogue that has been used to describe her.

Successful people cannot be offended because they know they are above most people.

Throughout my career as a Stuntman, I have had copious amounts of abuse hurled in my direction, has it ever affected me? NO, because I do not take it on board.

Nothing ruffles my feathers.

If you desire to be a Millionaire and be super successful you need to become bullet proof, you need to create for yourself your own set of rules, rules that enhance your life, not suppress it. Being different will make you rich, being different will make you successful.

Do as most people do in their mundane loser life and you will live a miserable existence and die broke.

If the direction you choose to go in is not challenged, then you certainly are not thinking and acting differently.

I am different, I am also very rich.

Be Different – **Write It Down.**

SUCCESSFUL PEOPLE HAVE SELF-DISCIPLINE

Self-discipline is a fantastic asset to have; this is one of your major drivers to success. Disciplined people Make It Happen, we write lists, set targets and goals, whatever we set out to do we achieve. No matter what obstacles are placed in our way we endure. If you are not disciplined you will fail, to be at the very top of your game being disciplined gets positive results.

To become a cabinet maker, I needed to be disciplined, same with Kung-Fu, every aspect revolves around discipline. Training to become a Stuntman I needed to be disciplined to train to obtain the skills required to gain acceptance onto the then stunt register. When running a thriving business, you need to be disciplined, same with finance, disciplined enough so you don't blow all your cash on hookers and cocaine and waste the rest. I train six days a week, no excuses, I train no matter what, in all weather, even extreme conditions; I am out there. I get results.

Adopt self-discipline into every aspect of your life, NO EXCUSES!

SUCCESSFUL PEOPLE WIN OR LEARN AND ACCEPT THAT

I can never lose, because I either win or I learn. Throughout our lives we make mistakes, wrong decisions, look back and wish we could turn back the clock; what we have to do is understand that is the roller coaster of life we are riding. I have got to a point in my life where I just do not care, if I mess up, I learn from it, I never think, I wish I had done that differently. I would not be a Millionaire today if I did things in a different manner, I am who I am, I am rebellious, outrageous and lawless.

I Win, I Learn, and I accept that. I do not dwell and nor should you, because that is a waste of energy, remember what you have previously read, focus your energy on the solution and NOT the problem.

It is satisfying when you win and it is even better when you learn, as by learning the very hard way you never make those foolish mistakes again.

SUCCESSFUL PEOPLE ARE RESILIENT

I have never witnessed an animal more resilient than a cat, strong, powerful, supple, intelligent and most of all independent. My Kung-Fu was developed from the study of animals and one of those animals is the tiger. Being resilient is a major asset in life even if you never desire to be wealthy and successful.

What resilience does is allow you to recover both mentally and physically from the challenges of life. Resilient people still feel the hurt and pain that life cruelty throws our way, however we do not stay sad for long. Yes, we have emotions, we cry; we accept and move on.

Throughout my life I have had to endure so much negativity, I take only positives from the very bad experiences I have encountered. I am resilient, I do not stay sad for long.

I pick myself up, dust myself down and carry on. I have developed problem-solving tools which I can call upon when needs must, which strengthen my resilient nature.

I have purpose, I always endure and so should you.

If you lose your job, and it so often happens in our volatile environment, focus on your future, use your motivation to find better, your resilience will aid you in appreciating what you have already achieved and help you steer your life in an even more productive direction.

Develop resilience – **Write It Down.**

SUCCESSFUL PEOPLE TAKE RESPONSIBILITY FOR THEIR ACTIONS

I mess up, My Fault!

I make mistakes, My Fault!

I take chances that sometimes do not work out, My Fault!

I take risks that sometimes result in trouble, My Fault!

Successful people take responsibility for their actions.

Now these are the traits of negative people:

Overweight, Somebody Else's Fault.

Broke, Somebody Else's Fault.

Lazy, Somebody Else's Fault.

Useless, Somebody Else's Fault.

Thick As Pig Shit, Somebody Else's Fault.

Unhealthy, Somebody Else's Fault.

I could go on and on, the Shit4Brainz in life never take responsibility for the constant Fuck Ups of their life. Never be that person. Successful people take responsibility for their actions, if they make errors, they learn from them and progress. We all make mistakes, until the last nail is driven hard into our coffin we always will.

Take responsibility and move on – **Write It Down.**

SUCCESSFUL PEOPLE ARE COMMITTED

Whatever I have set out to do in my life, no matter how outrageous, I have always achieved. In 1981 I joined the Air Training Corps, at school I was told I would give up, did I give up, NO, I enjoyed two amazing years. Whatever I set out to do I am committed, my career is a testament to that. If you want to be a Millionaire, you MUST be committed. I have a saying, 'Lazy Bastards Need Not Apply.' To be successful in every aspect of your life you have to first want, then apply yourself and be dedicated every day to working towards your chosen goal.
My career as a Stuntman takes immense commitment, and so has writing this book. I have to be committed. Look at the most successful wealthy people out there, they have committed themselves to being the best they can possibly be.

You want to be a Millionaire? Commit!

SUCCESSFUL PEOPLE ARE EXCELLENT AT GENERATING INCOME

In 1987 I read in a business magazine about digging ditches; the author had said that in between jobs he would dig ditches. He was not very well paid for this, however he found that by doing this it would motivate him to better himself as he hated the job.

Digging ditches was the motivation he needed, as digging on a cold damp day inspired him to realise he had to generate an income so vast that he would never have to dig a ditch again unless it was for himself.

There are income-generating businesses all around. Successful people seek those opportunities that others miss. As you are aware, in my cabinet-making days I generated an income by making things out of offcuts of wood and selling them. This supplemented my income and allowed me in time, as well as doing jobs on the side, to purchase my BMW outright with cash.

Remember what you read in Chapter 13 'Picks & Shovels', income generated from the gold rush. To be successful at whatever profession you choose or whatever venture you pursue you MUST excel at income generation.

There are so many opportunities all around you, astute businessmen like me seek out these all the time, no matter how wealthy we are, we love making money, we love securing a deal and the more you endure the better you become. Even if you start small by selling unwanted clothes, you are generating an income.

I firmly believe that unless you are really well paid you need a second income. Life has become so much more expensive, and our Bastard Corrupt Government has not made it any easier. Life at times can be shit, however it does not have to be that way.

Have several income streams and that way you make money while you sleep.

SUCCESSFUL PEOPLE HAVE GOOD PEOPLE AROUND THEM

I believe this one should apply to every aspect of your life, not just finance. Having good people around you is vital for your mental health. I sure know that when I dated the Ferrari without an engine, a 5 foot 11 inch model, who was as Thick As Pig Shit, an energy vampire, every aspect of my life suffered. Negative people only bring problems, they have to go, they are damaging!

You MUST have the right kind of people in your life. If you neglect this point you WILL suffer. Good people bring positive rewards; toxic people only bring trouble.

Successful people are happy to see you progress, they are willing to help and offer positive motivating advice, they do not suffer from that appalling disease worse than cancer by the name of jealousy. Good people will lift your spirits and, on those occasions when you are down, they will offer support.

Negative people love to see you fail, they thrive in a cesspit of negativity, because they are going nowhere fast. Never associate with the losers of life.

I am very selective about who I introduce into my world. If you do not meet my extremely high expectations, I will drop you just like you drop a stone into a pond; however, if you meet my very high standards, you will be a friend for life and I will help you.

Only have good people in your world – **Write It Down.**

Successful people are all cut from the same cloth, remember that.

SUCCESSFUL PEOPLE KNOW THEIR VALUE

You have to know your worth. I charge an extremely high daily rate for my stunt work and also my public speaking, because I Know My Worth. In 1997 I was working in Scotland on a BBC drama entitled *Looking After JoJo* starring Robert Carlyle. I had just announced what my daily rate was as an Intermediate Stuntman, which was much higher even than established Stunt Co-ordinators were charging.

I was met with anger, not support or well done, just extreme negativity and disbelief. 'What makes you think you are better than us?' I was asked. Only one other Stuntman supported me. What I had done was established that I never wanted to be an average Stuntman, I was exceptional.

Let's look at it this way. Why is it that Lamborghini charge a premium for their cars? So do Ferrari, how many people could afford a Lamborghini or a Ferrari? Very few, so why do their cars cost the hundreds of thousands of pounds that they do? Because they know their worth, they know what they represent and that warrants a premium.

I set out my stall in a very productive way, I bring value and that value comes with a hefty price tag, I am reliable, I can do exactly what I say I can do.

I am a problem solver and that comes at a cost. Sometimes in life one has to pay a premium. I reside in an exclusive area of England, I live in a hamlet, to reside here I had to pay a premium to live in such luxury. Being in such tranquil surroundings makes my life more productive than if I lived in a city. I value my mental and physical health and so should you.

By knowing your value, you can charge a very high fee for your services, PROVIDED you can **Walk The Walk,** it is no good if you are good at **Talking The Talk,** as the saying goes, you have no lead in your pencil.

When you know your value and your worth you will be in demand and set up for life.

This leads me on to a very interesting and valuable story about ATTITUDE, and a very bad one at that. My fiancée treated me to a surprise cream tea at Burghley House in Lincolnshire, which should have been an enjoyable occasion; however, it was ruined by a staff member's arrogant attitude that led to my fiancée taking Burghley House to court and securing a victory.

The booking was made online and a vegetarian cream tea was ordered for me. When we arrived, the tablecloth was stained and there were these shitty Christmas crackers on the table and no staff member knew what The Fuck they were doing. We were told that it was the first time Burghley House had undertaken to offer a cream tea Christmas experience, and things were not going to plan.

Let's wind this one back a little. How Fucking hard is it to put on a cream tea? Obviously very hard, for the incompetent staff at Burghley House. I was presented with a vegan cream tea, NOT a vegetarian one, as my fiancée had ordered. We complained, only to be told that there were many problems on the day, and as the manager was not present, we were assured that if we emailed in our issue, it would be resolved to our satisfaction.

Well, it was not; because of ARROGANCE our complaint was referred to as Feedback and at no point did the events manager, Carla, ever take our complaint seriously, stating that she was not going to provide us with a refund.

The cream tea cost £42.50 each. My fiancée had consumed hers as she had ordered the meat option, my vegetarian option was wrongly replaced with vegan food; one cannot do this. Burghley House claimed that they had provided me with an adequate alternative.

Now how difficult is it to provide a stand of vegetarian sandwiches? It would take less than five minutes to do so, NOT slap some vegan food down at our table and think that was acceptable because the catering staff are too Fucking lazy to provide a vegetarian option.

So, if one had ordered a tin of Poppy Red paint and on collection it had been replaced with Pillar Box Red, would that be acceptable? If one was told that was an adequate alternative because it is still red paint?

So, you can see that by having no business acumen whatsoever in resolving a genuine customer complaint Carla's arrogant bad attitude landed Burghley House in court.

Now if she had any business acumen, she would have first apologised for not providing what my fiancée had lawfully paid for, and secondly, she could have offered us free a cream tea for two, demonstrating that Burghley House could provide us with a better experience. She could have even offered a refund of £42.50, she did nothing, only stated in every reply that she was not going to refund.

We filed a County Court claim against Burghley House as this was the only way we could resolve this.

We agreed to mediation offered through the court services and yes, you guessed, Carla did not show up.

Off to court we went, and yet again Carla did not show. The Arrogant Bitch!

The outcome cost Burghley House £186. They were found guilty in their absence of being in breach of the Consumer Rights Act 2015 and ordered to pay within 21 days.

Now a simple customer complaint that could have been handled better resulted in Burghley House having to pay £186 for their arrogant attitude. Arrogance will destroy you! Just like it destroyed the reputation of Burghley House, which has lost them business, and they now have a County Court Judgment hanging over their sorry asses for the next six years.
So now you have read and absorbed the characteristics of successful people, how many of these do you already possess?

You now need to focus on the ones you lack and create your action plan so that each day you develop the positive winning attitude you will need to become a Millionaire.

Chapter 21

The Pension Trap

Can you recall in Chapter 15 I said I would elaborate on why you SHOULD NOT have a pension, which I also covered in my amazing book *With Confidence* and here are the reasons why.

Pensions were created around the 1700s; by that I mean private pensions, as government pensions do go back further, to 1590. The first was to support disabled seamen. I am going to completely separate the government state pension and private pensions.

Originally this is how a private pension functioned.

Workers and individuals paid in at one end, either through a weekly contribution from their wages or by taking out a pension with a provider. This money went into a pot to increase and make money out of the contributor's money, are you following this?

One could draw on their pension from the age of 55, take a lump sum and receive a monthly payout. Life expectancy was predicted that one would be long gone by the age of 75. So, for a pension to be successful you first need enough people contributing.

Secondly you need the investment pot to grow, this needs to grow as this, and the people who contribute, pay those who have retired, simple as, however, the reality is this.

Not enough people are now contributing; most cannot afford to and those that do are far too stupid to understand the process. If they studied the principle of how the pension system needs to work, they would not get involved. With low interest rates and world instability the pot is not growing, it is actually having the opposite effect and shrinking. One also has to be mindful that fees are deducted from the contributor, these fees pay the provider's employees.

The good news is that people are living much longer, so have received monthly pension payouts for a duration greater than that for which the structure was originally intended. So, to put it to you as directly as I can, I am no Carol Vodaphone, however, with my very limited ability with maths I can deduce that the pension system is antiquated.

So why do people still contribute?

Here is your answer:

Because they are just what our corrupt government needs them to be.

Model Citizens.

Mediocre

Obedient

Dependent

Entertained

Lifeless

Are you one of these?

Most people are Sheeple, they just follow the crowd, do not have the courage to forge their own way in life. Read the small print... It states clearly that your investment can also lose money; that you may lose part or all of your investment. Today pensions are a gamble I am not willing to take. I do not have one as I do not have any faith in what they now represent.

The government are begging you to invest in one so they can exonerate themselves from all responsibility for you when you retire and, get a load of this, you get taxed on them, yes, the money you have paid in is taxable.

Doomed to fail. If I gave you £50,000, would you like to have full control of it or would you hand it over to a complete stranger to invest for you? Have the Confidence and Courage to be in full control of your life. – **Write It Down.**

To be super successful and financially secure you MUST be The Shepherd and NOT the sheep. Have you noticed that the people who are Piss Poor are the ones who not only moan about how shit their life is, they also are the ones who obey every instruction our corrupt government barks at them. That is exactly why they are Piss Poor, and they are far too stupid to realise it.

The aim of my book is to provide you with what actually works to make you rich. You now have a solid foundation to structure your finances in a simple way so you are fully aware of every penny coming in and every penny going out and this is how to do it.

Now today so many people neglect having a paper bank statement posted to them. This is a very bad move and if you are one of them, stop right now. You MUST have your bank statements in paper format, and you MUST scrutinise them to establish if they are correct. This becomes your Monthly Money Management.

Monthly Money Management. – Write It Down.

I have everything in paper format. I do not do online banking, I deal in cash whenever possible and I know exactly when money is coming in and when money is going out, I manage my money well and you should too. No online receipts, again everything in paper format. It is the only way.

Another important point is never to have a credit card. You know my feelings on borrowing money, if you want something then work hard for it, that way you will appreciate it much more than having to meet a credit card debt once a month.

If you have appreciating assets, they will reward you more than any pension ever could, and these are the reasons why.

As you are aware, our Bastard government tax you on your pension, they tax you on earnings you have already paid tax on, how fucked up is that!

THEY SET YOU UP TO FAIL.

Classic vehicles are listed as Wasted Assets, meaning that the moment they are driven off the dealer's forecourt they instantly lose value. Through time vehicles drop in price to a point where they bottom out and remain that way for several years.

If the vehicle is exceptional in some way, be that a rare example or is in concours condition with very low mileage, it will appreciate in value. However, on paper it will be worthless, meaning that when you come to sell it you will not have to pay capital gains tax and the money you receive is yours, tax free. How cool is that, unlike a pension where you are subject to tax.

Now there is a point I need to stress. Classic vehicle prices are currently very high as I write this in 2025. If you are going to venture down that road you need to purchase the best vehicle you can possibly afford, one that does not require any restoration, nurture it, enjoy it and in time it will reward you.

I know more about Lamborghinis than any other vehicle, they have been my passion for many years.

In 2009 a Lamborghini Silhouette would cost you £42,000 which equates to £73,000 today.

That very same car today would cost you £145,000, making you a hefty £103,000 profit; now is that not better than a pension? That is why having a Wasted Asset in your portfolio is vital and why I DO NOT and WILL NEVER have a pension, I do not need one.

I will be entitled to the state pension, however our Bastard government has robbed me of around £20,000 by moving my state pension age from

The Pension Trap

65 to 67. Now can you see why I hate the government so much? The fuckers just want you dead.

In 2009 a Lamborghini Countach would have cost you £55,000, which equates to £95,000 today. That very same car today would cost you £700,000, making you a hefty £645,000 profit TAX FREE. You also get the pleasure of owning a Lamborghini.

Start small, check out the classifieds and look up classic and supercars, also attend car shows and learn your craft, build relationships up with owners and you could bag yourself a cracking deal. This is how classics and supercars change hands, relationships are formed, and from that business deals are struck in the friendliest of environments.

Never fall into the Pensions Trap. If you do, you will live to regret it, there are much better options out there to secure your future, investments that YOU control, NOT a provider.

Pensions are antiquated. Move forward, controlling your life, work hard, work smart, adapt to your life everything you have absorbed from Chapter 20 and you will in time become a Millionaire.

Chapter 22

You Can Take A Horse To Water

You can take a horse to water, but you cannot make it drink.

How true are those very words. You can give a person all the tools and help they need to make them a much better person, to make them successful, to help them develop their life, provide them with a structure to become a Millionaire, yet if they are not thirsty enough to drink you are wasting your time.

I have tried to help several people over the years; I have sat down with them, explained to them what they need to do and what they MUST stop doing to have a much more rewarding and financially secure life and then I am met with:

It won't work.

It will fail.

I won't win.

I will give up.

Those kinds of people place no value on what they have before them.

The kind of people I am referring to are those individuals who sit there feeling sorry for themselves saying, "I wish life was better." Well, get off your Fat Lazy Ass and make it better. Some people think they have problems when what they really need is a Wake-up Call.

I became a Millionaire without any help whatsoever. I motivated myself, and remember, in the 1980s I was foraging through bins for food to survive and today I have the most amazing life ever, all created by my thirst for success.

Are you thirsty? Are you hungry? You need to be.

If you are not, you will not have the drive required to become a Millionaire. Even though I am financially secure I love making money, I still have that hunger and I still have that thirst.

Attitude Is Everything.

Remember, NEVER concern yourself with what anyone thinks of you, good or bad. You must be Self-Motivated and hard-working, you see those words HARD WORK resonate throughout my writing, for very good reason.

Does a person who regularly works out, trains every day, eats a good diet, has a routine, NOT get results? No, it does not happen that way. If you work hard, you get results. It may take time, however, if you are consistent, you WILL get positive results and the same can be said of finance.

Money Makes Money and Knowledge is Power.

You now have the knowledge; do you have what it takes to be super successful and a Millionaire?

Let's Find Out!

WAYS TO EARN MONEY THROUGH EMPLOYMENT

Employed

This is normally the natural choice when one leaves school or further education, it is by far the easiest option. For some this is a comfortable and somewhat secure decision, however I must stress there is no longer a

'Job For Life', those days are long gone, when a person would leave school, become a bank clerk and work their way up to becoming a bank manager. Job security no longer exists. Your income tax and national insurance is taken at source and what you have left in your pay packet is yours.

You travel to and from work under your own steam and work the set hours your job requires, being provided with holiday and sick pay.

Self-Employed

For myself, leaving school and becoming a cabinet maker, I was employed at Thomas Pearson. However, the period of six years was not wasted. I learned valuable skills that allowed me to become self-employed. A fine example again of being resourceful.

Someone selling fruit and vegetables from a market stall would be classed as self-employed.

A self-employed person is allowed to claim business expenses which reduces their income tax bill, also they pay far less national insurance. However, they must find their own work. This can be off-putting to those out there who demand an easy life. Unless you are the director of a conglomerate you will struggle to become a Millionaire through employment.

Yes, there are the exceptions, such as film stars and rock stars, however these are very rare examples and working in the television and film industry myself, most of the high earners I have encountered have no business acumen whatsoever and end up pissing the lot up the nearest wall.

Let's just refer back to Chapter 20 and examine the following:

Successful people have an aim.

Successful people mix with positive people.

Successful people know what they want.

Successful people are not shy.

Successful people create their own set of rules.

Successful people manage their money well.

Successful people are good at receiving compliments.

Successful people tend to be very brave.

Successful people are consistently learning and progressing.

Successful people admire other rich and successful people.

Successful people always create opportunities.

Successful people focus on the solution not the problem.

Successful people believe in their ability.

Successful people have a positive mental attitude.

Successful people are different.

Successful people have self-discipline.

Successful people win or learn and accept that.

Successful people are resilient.

Successful people take responsibility for their actions.

Successful people are committed.

Successful people are excellent at generating income.

Successful people have good people around them.

Successful people know their value.

These are all the characteristics of a super successful self-employed business owner, because to be successful one has to have what it takes and if you lack what it takes you need not bother.

Life is hard, no matter what, unexpected barriers are gonna be put in your way, you MUST condition yourself for these unpredictable times.

You need to be aggressive; you also need to HATE.

Now I see hate as a positive; hate is a driver towards success. I hated school; my coping strategy consisted of a chart on my bedroom wall with every day of that year I had to attend school. Once I returned home at the end of the day, I would cross off the day, the week, the month, my leaving day of the 27 May 1983 was my inspiration. I never went back to collect my exam results and they are probably still sitting in the school reception to this day. They can stay there, as even back in 1983 I was determined to be successful without a piece of paper saying otherwise.

I created a chart when I was training to become a Stuntman, you must have a plan and a purpose.

A Plan and a Purpose – **Write It Down.**

In 1990 I was offered a job as a cabinet maker in Derby. Sadly, Derby is a right shit hole, however that is another book. I took the job and hated it; I hated every second I was there. I used HATE as a tool to better myself. I looked around and established that I could do better and that is exactly what I did. HATE is an amazing driver, I did not moan or complain, I got off my ass and established my very own cabinet-making and joinery business.

Ignore the Shit4Brainz in life that say hate is bad and one should not hate; HATE is a motivator for positive change.

If you HATE IT – CHANGE IT – **Write It Down.**

I can provide you with all the help and advice that WILL make you a Millionaire. What I cannot do is decide what business your wealth is going to be created through, that is your choice and your choice alone.

What I can tell you is this, work hard, work smart, adopt the traits of a successful person into your life and you will receive rewards both financially and emotionally.

If I had not had self-belief and yearned for a better life I would not have the amazing life I have today. Hate was an amazing driver to my success.

I created my Own Set Of Rules for my life and I live by them every day. Hard work pays off every time!

How's that vision board looking?

As I write this, I am looking at my vision board in my study. I still keep cuttings of various Lamborghinis and beautiful homes I now own, alongside all the Tits & Fanny adorning the board too, I have no idea how they got there, if I find out you will be the first to know.

This chapter began with these words:

YOU CAN TAKE A HORSE TO WATER BUT YOU CANNOT MAKE IT DRINK.

Now over to you. You have invested your time wisely so far, now is the time for you to put what you have learned into action and create your many income streams.

Always be Professional

By that I mean invest in a professional email address NOT any of the following:

Hotmail
Yahoo
Gmail
AOL

If I see a business with any of the above as their email address, they DO NOT win my business. If they cannot be bothered to purchase a professional email address what does that say about their reputation? It tells me they are shit! No business acumen whatsoever.

You also need to ditch Facefuck and Twatter now known as X.

What exactly are you doing broadcasting your life to the whole world? Most of them do not even give a shit and most others are not intelligent to give a shit because they have Shit4Brainz anyway.

Wake Up, get yourself off shitty lowlife websites like Facefuck and Twatter. They are Pure Poison, The Cesspit of the world, they do far more harm than they do good, you should be far better than that if you aspire to be a Millionaire.

Also have a professional well-managed and maintained website, created by a web designer, NOT your friend's sister's next-door neighbour's window cleaner who is allegedly making websites on the side.

If you care to view a professional, well-constructed, award-winning website, check out www.fallingforyou.tv

Also have a landline telephone number and your mobile telephone number available for your potential customers to be able to contact you and an answering machine with your voice on it.

Also learn how to write your mobile telephone number correctly, this one amazes me just how as Thick As Pig Shit some people can be when they are totally Fucking Clueless in layout.

Your mobile number consists of 00000 000000 11 digits, first five then a space followed by the last six. Can that be any simpler? NOT 00000000000.

Again, when I see a mobile number not laid out correctly a company sure is not securing my business, I just think if you are not capable of getting the basics right what will your standard of work be like? SHIT!

Always reply to emails, even if it is to say NO; this is an absolute must. I work in by far the most bad-mannered and rude industry one could encounter; most producers are forgetful, bad-mannered and liars, sadly that is how films and television programmes are made.

Do Not be one of those kinds of people, you are better than that.

Politeness Pays Off – **Write It Down.**

Also, your business year MUST start on 1 January and end on the 31 December, NOT the fucked-up way our corrupt government want it from 6 April onwards. Who came up with the tax year anyway? They must have been as Thick As Pig Shit!

A year is a year END OF!

You must also have the confidence to speak your mind, no matter how controversial, remember it will be you who puts food on the table. We live in the most pathetic of times with WOKEism and Diversity Shit.

When you come to employ people, they MUST be able to do the job, MERIT is all that matters NOT how diverse they are.

Do you want diversity in Bomb Disposal? I certainly DO NOT.

You MUST NOT be influenced by another person's thoughts or opinions.

This brings me onto a famous tale which was aimed at young children, although its value resonates so well with today's "sheeple' society. It is called 'Chicken Licken'.

I was first introduced to this in a Ladybird book while at Infant school. Mum would read it to my brother and I before we would go to bed. However, Mum never told us the real ending. Ironically when talking about my childhood with my fiancée she bought me the Ladybird book so I could read the uncensored version, and it made me realise just how influenced some people can be.

To condense the story an acorn drops onto Chicken Licken's head, and he believes the sky is falling. He needed to go and tell the king, and along the way he meets with a hen, cock, duck, drake, goose and a turkey, who all accompany him to tell the king that the sky is falling.

They then meet a fox, telling him that the sky is falling and they are going to inform the king.

The fox says he knows a short cut that will take them straight to the king, they all follow and become the fox family's dinner.

Now when I re-read this it reminded me of the bollocks we are fed on a near daily basis by government and media about non-existent climate change and that the Chicken Lickens of this world actually believe it. Never be one of those 'Sheeple' of life who cannot cut it in the real world and are far too fuckin stupid to make money.

Again, think who is putting food on the table, who is working smart and hard? YOU! Fuck Em!

You MUST:

GO OUT THERE NOW AND MAKE IT HAPPEN!

REMEMBER, BE PREPARED FOR HARD WORK.

Chapter 23

You Are Your BEST Investment!

You are fully aware that you need to invest in your financial education, be that reading books, magazines or viewing entrepreneurial videos, you also need to invest in your health.

You work hard to accumulate your wealth to become a Millionaire and you are in such poor heath that you cannot enjoy your rewards. I have witnessed this so much throughout my life.

From the age of 17 I have worked out on a near-daily basis If the body is strong, the mind is stronger. No excuses, I train!

Exercising on a daily basis is vital. You must create for yourself, if you do not already do so, a Monday through to Friday training routine. No excuses.

Now I am not expecting you to do a two-hour training routine a day as I do. I have to be in peak physical condition as a Stuntman and for my Kung-Fu. I also really enjoy the positive results training brings, those endorphins are amazing, they are one of my many motivators.

Good diet, daily exercise and lots of sleep are vital for a happy, heathy positive life.

You MUST invest in yourself – **Write It Down.**

However you take these words is purely your choice:

Go out on any given day and observe just how many Lazy Bastards are out there, the obese and the clinically obese and our Shit4Brainz government think a sugar tax is the answer and if one even suggests that these Lazy Bastards are abnormal, one is deemed to be 'Fat Shaming' another one of our W.O.K.E. sayings that we have been subjected to.

I care not what people think of me as I am sure reading this far you are aware, what is apparent is I am correct in what I say, there is a shocking obesity problem out there and it is all down to certain individuals being lazy.

If you move more and eat less you will lose weight, WILL POWER!

You need to be motivated to establish your many income-generating schemes. I truly believe if a person is together, organised, reliable and driven and works hard they will not fall into the 'Lazy Bastard' category, because they will be burning the calories to succeed.

As you read in Chapter Two, I walked the streets to post my job applications to the many carpentry and joinery businesses in Nottingham and by having this hard-working ethos I Make Things Happen!

I do not moan or complain, I take action. I dislike lazy people who blame their failing on other people. So, you make your plan, your training plan, create a programme that works for you and be DEDICATED. It is pointless having unlimited wealth and not having the good health to enjoy it.

You have to Move To Improve – **Write It Down.**

Also, I must stress, do not join a gym. They are a complete waste of money. You can get yourself fit and in shape with everything you have around you at home and outside.

You should be using your own body weight in the form of press-ups, pull-ups and sit-ups, all done correctly, and get yourself a skipping rope, a speed rope that looks like it was made from a washing line, they are the best.

Eventually when you have created your wealth, you can have a home gym.

You also need to be mentally strong alongside your physical health, no volume of money in the world means anything if you are depressed. If you have not already done so, read my self-help book, *With Confidence*. After reading that you will view your life and your world in a much more positive way.

I do not want to hear any excuses for why you cannot train both your body and your mind. I hear so much negativity, and I view so much negativity on a near-daily basis as to why someone claims they cannot do the most basic of activities.

The blame gamers of our sad pathetic world.

I have exploited my full potential in life through my thoughts, dreams, vision, abilities and attitude to **Make It Happen!** and So Can You.

Becoming wealthy is a choice, being fit is a choice, having a positive outlook on your life and your future is a choice. As you are aware, my start in life was not good, I never moaned or complained, I had a choice and that choice was to take positive action to make my life the absolute best it could possibly be.

Now no matter just how much wealth I accumulate, I am willing to learn, to educate myself, because I Am My Best Investment and do you know what? You are too.

You will always achieve what you believe to add value to your life.

You MUST Make YOU matter – **Write It Down.**

Resilience is going to be one of your greatest assets.

Be 'The Master Of Your Own Success' – **Write It Down.**

You have to Make A Difference by Being Different!

Now remember what you read at the very beginning of my book:

HOW TO MAKE THIS BOOK WORK FOR YOU

I requested that you wrote down key points in a notebook, and if you did follow exactly as you were meant to, you will have 70 vital resources that you can refer to along your journey to becoming a Millionaire. You can yourself keep adding your own thoughts to the list as this is about you, your life and your future.

I possessed the power to change my life and so can you. Build your mindset like a fortress that cannot be destroyed. You were created to STAND OUT, not fit in.

Once you experience what freedom feels like there is no going back, it is one of the most amazing feelings ever. Remember, we were never educated at school to be successful, school was our first waste of time.

Time is your greatest asset, so do not ever waste it as it can never be replaced.

Use every piece of negativity towards you as 'Fuel For Your Fire' and remember if you tame a Wolf when it is young it becomes a pet.

Never go through your life trying to seek approval and existing just to please the weak.

Think of life as Alcatraz. Some prisoners decorate the walls of their cells and call it home; those exceptional individuals direct their energy into digging tunnels and seeking freedom.

So go out there and invest in yourself and remember for all the toxicity that will be directed towards you when you flaunt your success, just say to yourself these very words.

Fuck Em!

www.ingramcontent.com/pod-product-compliance
Lightning Source LLC
Chambersburg PA
CBHW020357170426
43200CB00005B/206